Middle East Burning

Mark Hitchcock

HARVEST HOUSE PUBLISHERS

EUGENE, OREGON

Cover by Left Coast Design, Portland, Oregon

Cover photo © Trinacria Photo / Shutterstock

Published in association with William K. Jensen Literary Agency, 119 Bampton Court, Eugene, Oregon 97404.

MIDDLE EAST BURNING
Copyright © 2012 by Mark Hitchcock
Published by Harvest House Publishers
Eugene, Oregon 97402
www.harvesthousepublishers.com

Library of Congress Cataloging-in-Publication Data
Hitchcock, Mark.
Middle East burning / Mark Hitchcock.
        p. cm.
ISBN 978-0-7369-3996-6 (pbk.)
ISBN 978-0-7369-4260-7 (eBook)
1. Bible—Prophecies—Middle East. 2. Arab-Israeli conflict—Biblical teaching.
3. Bible—Prophecies—End of the world. I. Title.
BS649.N45H58 2012
236′.9—dc23

                                                    2011024055

Printed in the United States of America

12 13 14 15 16 17 18 19 20 / LB-SK / 10 9 8 7 6 5 4 3 2 1

To Gary Spencer
With gratitude for your faithful friendship and
the delightful gift of encouragement you
give to me and my family.

Contents

Our world is on fire, and man without God will never be able to control the flames. The demons of hell have been let loose. The fires of passion, greed, hate, and lust are sweeping the world. We seem to be plunging madly toward Armageddon...The world has been in flames before, but only in a limited sense. Today our world is a common neighborhood, all of it reachable in mere hours by physical flight and in seconds over the airwaves. This accessibility increases the spread of tension and dissension. Thus when the fires of war and lawlessness break out, they leap the national boundaries and cultural differences to become major conflagrations. The whole world is filled with riots, demonstrations, threats, wars...This is the generation destined to live in the midst of crisis, danger, fear, and death. We are like a people under sentence of death, waiting for the date to be set. We sense that something is about to happen.[1]

BILLY GRAHAM, *WORLD AFLAME (1965)*

Chapter 1

Arab Spring...or Fall?

*The turmoil in Tunisia, Egypt, Libya, Yemen, Bahrain,
Oman and Syria (and you ain't seen nothing yet...),
coupled with the expected U.S. evacuation from
Iraq and Afghanistan, the Iranian threat and the
inherent non-reliability of international or Western
guarantees and forces do not usher in Spring; they do
usher in lethal geo-political twisters and floods.*[1]

YORAM ETTINGER

*Democracy is like a streetcar. You ride it until you
get to your destination and then you get off.*[2]

TURKISH PRIME MINISTER RECIP TAYYIP ERDOGAN

*It is still too early to tell whether the waves of change
sweeping over the shores of North Africa and the
Middle East will erode the foundations of autocracy
or, conversely, whether they will merely substitute secular
authoritarianism with Islamist totalitarianism.*[3]

ALI ALFONEH, *THE JERUSALEM POST*

The headlines during the spring months of 2011 said it all:

"Apocalypse Now: Tsunamis. Earthquakes. Nuclear Meltdowns. Revolutions. Economies on the Brink. What the #@%! Is Next?"[4]

"The Revolution"[5]

"Fire from Egypt and Tunisia Flames Across Arab World"[6]

"Where Is the Next Upheaval?"[7]

"The Middle East Crisis Has Just Begun"[8]

"Why Is the Middle East Burning and Can Anyone Put Out the Fire?"[9]

"Gaddafi's Last Stand"[10]

"A World Turned Upside Down"[11]

It all began with one tiny spark on December 17, 2010. This spark ignited the blazing brush fire that is now raging across the Middle East. It started when an unemployed Tunisian, Mohamed Bouazizi, doused himself with paint thinner and lit a match. This desperate act of self-immolation was apparently due to the embarrassment and humiliation he suffered after the government confiscated apples he was selling so he could support his family. To make matters worse, Bouazizi was slapped in the face and publicly beaten twice. When his trip to the governor's office was rebuffed, he believed he had been completely stripped of his dignity, so in a final act of despair he lit a match that ignited a revolution that has since reverberated throughout the Middle East.

Bouazizi's action ignited street clashes that inspired nearly a dozen other men to set themselves on fire in Egypt, Algeria, and Mauritania and ultimately toppled the autocratic regime of Tunisia, which had been led by Zine el-Abidine Ben Ali. The rage continues to spread across the Middle East, and dictators in the region are feeling the heat. We've all seen the disturbing images of mayhem emanating from the Arab nations with no discernible end in sight. There are lulls and interruptions, but the future is uncertain. The explosive events have shocked, surprised, and stunned the world. The question on the minds of many people is this: Will the present wave of uprisings bring about new democracies in the Middle East, perhaps ones that are more friendly to the West and more benevolent to their own people? Will nations like Egypt become more moderate and remain at peace with Israel? Or will this swelling tide clear the way for radical Islamic leaders to take control of these nations—leaders who are even more oppressive than their predecessors and want to impose Islamic sharia law?

Domino-effect Revolutions

I live in Oklahoma, where the "wind comes sweepin' down the plains." At no time is that more true than in the spring. The gusty winds are great for wind power, but terrible when there's been a drought and a stray spark ends up igniting a grass fire. When these fires are whipped by the winds, they turn into vicious, unpredictable infernos that consume everything in their path.

Today, there is a blazing inferno sweeping across the Middle East. The winds of revolution are whipping up the flames and no one seems to know what's going to happen or where it's all headed. After the initial flash in Tunisia, it took just 28 days for Tunisian president Zine el-Abidine Ben Ali to be sent packing to Saudi Arabia after 23 years of tyranny. The winds then blew the glowing embers to Egypt, the most powerful and populous nation in the Arab world. And from there the flames have continued to spread. Nations are erupting "like a line of dormant volcanoes into revolutionary rioting."[12]

When the flames spread to Egypt and began what is now known as the January 25th Revolution, a watching world was captivated day after day as newscasts showed scenes of thousands of emboldened protesters and rioters marching, shouting, and camping in the shadow of the famed Egyptian Museum. The Egyptians stood their ground in Tahrir Square and demanded the ouster of Hosni Mubarak, who had ruled Egypt with absolute power for 30 years. After an intense 18-day revolution, Mubarak finally succumbed to the deafening outcry and walked away in shame on February 11, 2011. An interim military regime was appointed, and as of this writing, Egypt's future is unsettled and uncertain, and elections are allegedly in the offing.

From there, the flames continued to spread. They were stoked in Morocco, Algeria, Jordan, Libya, Bahrain, Oman, Yemen, Iran, Syria, and even Saudi Arabia. Protests convulsed the Middle East over long-suppressed, long-ignored grievances. Dictators who had lived large on the backs of the masses were either sent scurrying for cover or quickly and brutally suppressed those who dared to take part in public demonstrations.

In Libya, when strongman dictator Colonel Muammar Abu Minyar al-Gaddafi (also spelled Qaddafi) and his tyrannical regime came under siege from rebel forces, they struck back with a vengeance. The nation quickly descended into "a patchwork of liberated zones and violently defended redoubts of the regime."[13] For a while it appeared Gaddafi would defeat the rebels. Finally, the UN and NATO stepped in to stem the slaughter, giving rebels a brief reprieve, but a long standoff ensued. Most alarming to the West, Libya's 1.2 million barrels of oil a day was taken off-line and oil prices quickly spiked as uncertainty mushroomed. Prices at the pump rose 20 percent over the period of just a few weeks, exposing the West's ongoing vulnerability to any slight disruption in oil supply. Gaddafi was finally deposed on August 29, 2011, then killed on October 20, 2011.

Arab Awakening

The series of uprisings in the Middle East has been dubbed the "Arab Spring." Many have hailed it as an Arab awakening and applauded the protests expressing a desire for freedom and democracy. While freedom and democracy are great gifts and should be desired and fostered by all people, the explanation for the recent rash of uprisings may not be all that simple. Additional factors appear to be lurking behind the scenes of the wave of protests and anger that have engulfed the Middle East and North Africa. Among these forces are "the global financial crisis, rising costs of living, high unemployment—especially of educated youth, frustration from decades of living under authoritarian and corrupt regimes, various document leaks revealing more details about how governments around the world are dealing and viewing each other."[14] Of course, for many caught up in the unrest a desire for democracy may be their chief goal and motivation, but we are naïve if we fail to recognize that the real impetus behind the so-called Arab Spring could be much deeper and much more sinister.

According to Wikileaks founder Julian Assange, the uprisings are "a direct result of the website's dumping of classified documents about each country's leadership."[15] One of Assange's document dumps of classified internal Israeli documents revealed "surprisingly intimate levels of cooperation between Israel and the Arab governments now under fire."[16]Assange told Israel's Yediot Ahronot: "The documents we released in the past few months were the fuel that ignited the Arab revolts."[17] According to good sources,

> He explained that Wikileaks began publishing the secret U.S. Embassy cables on November 29, 2010, in Arab newspapers, including Lebanon's Al-Akhbar, which eventually made their way to North Africa, Saudi Arabia, and Lebanon, which led to the eruption of the popular revolts. For example, one cable from the U.S. Embassy in Tel Aviv documented a private talk between Bahrain's King Sheikh Hamad ibn Isa Al Khalifa and the U.S. Ambassador in which the Ambassador reported: "He [the king] revealed that Bahrain already has contacts with Israel at the intelligence/security level (with Mossad) and indicated that Bahrain will be willing to move forward in other areas."

> Assange isn't merely blowing his own horn on the impact the document dump has had across the Middle East. One need only look at the governments most at risk. Their repressive policies may have sparked the early revolts, but it was their secret *collusion with the United States and with Israel* that sustained it and provided it with fuel. The documents showed that some

Arab leaders didn't hate Israel and America. At least, not as much as their populations wanted them to. That is what Arab Spring is *really* all about. "Death to America." "Death to Israel." To millions of ordinary Arab citizens, they aren't just slogans. It was the *reason* that they put up with their repressive regimes—they believed that their leaders hated the two Satans as much as they did.[18]

The article continues:

> The Egyptians didn't come out in mass demonstrations against Hosni Mubarak because they hunger for Western-style democracy like that of America or Israel. It was over Mubarak's relationship with the United States and Israel as revealed by the Wikileaks dump. The same holds true across the rest of the Middle East. The more the government was revealed to have cooperated with Israel or America, the more restive the population and tenuous that government's hold on power.[19]

The handwriting is on the wall concerning who will ultimately take over in Egypt and other Middle Eastern nations, and it won't be the forces of democracy. Roger Wiegand warns,

> Any political change of power, especially by force, will not be in the direction of a Western vision of Democracy. Radical Islam is what is forcing the change, so any new governing power structure will have to recognize the radicals and include them in a new regime. Once they officially have a foot in the political governing

door, it is not a large step to take control of the entire country.[20]

What we are witnessing could well be the embryonic, emerging Islamic caliphate that jihadists want. The tide of revolution could eventually usher into power states with radical leaders who want to establish sharia law the same way it was implanted in Iran after the revolution in 1979. These developments could light the fuse to the Middle East powder keg and trigger the military conflict predicted in Ezekiel 38–39.

It's Not the Same Old Middle East

While some of these uprisings, such as those in Syria, may be temporarily stuffed and stalled by bullets, the people of the Middle East are more aware today of what's going on in the outside world than at any other time and have more resources available to them. While there is still widespread illiteracy and poverty in all Islamic Middle East nations, there is a burgeoning sector of the population that is educated and technology savvy. Social networking websites have played a key role in the uprisings, especially in Egypt. The "Facebook Generation" has already been given much of the credit for the overthrow of Hosni Mubarak. The Egyptian government blocked Internet use in an effort to throw water on the flames of revolt, but to no avail, and Egyptian Google executive Wael Ghonim was the darling of Tahrir Square on January 27, 2011.

Information technology, however, is a powerful resource not only for the promoters of democracy, but also the enemies of freedom. Fouad X, the head of information technology for Hezbollah in Lebanon, uses email and the Internet to recruit young Islamists willing to serve their "sacred cause." The continuing expansion of Internet technology will continue to play a major role, for both good and evil, as the flames of unrest continue to spread. As Niall Ferguson notes, "The clash of civilizations would have been easy for the West to win if it had simply pitted the ideas and institutions of the 21st century against those of the seventh. No such luck. In the new mash of civilizations, our most dangerous foes are the Islamists who understand how to post *fatwas* on Facebook, email the holy Quran, and tweet the call to jihad."[21]

So technology will clearly have a key role in the future of the Middle East and the global balance of power. This is another key sign of the times as the world "shrinks" and the globalism envisioned in Revelation chapters 13 and 17 comes to fruition.

Filling the Void

In November 2008, during a *Wall Street Journal* forum, former White House chief of staff Rahm Emanuel was quoted as saying, "You never want a serious crisis to go to waste. And what I mean by that is an opportunity to do things you think you could not do before." His stunningly opportunistic statement was a transparent and honest admission of the Obama administration's tactical approach to crises. The employment of this perspective has reaped a sea-change of initiatives in the US during a time of extended economic difficulties. However, our trials, tribulations, and turmoil pale in comparison to what is happening in the Middle East today. Opportunities abound for evil forces to exploit the uprisings to their advantage.

According to *The Economist*,

> The latest issue of *Inspire*, an on-line jihadist magazine that declares itself the English-language mouthpiece of al-Qaeda in the Arabian Peninsula, the Yemen-based franchise of Osama bin Laden's global jihadist group, hails the Arab's revolutionary fervour as a golden opportunity. "The revolutions that are shaking the thrones of dictators are good for the Muslims, good for the mujahideen and bad for the imperialists of the West and their henchman in the Muslim world."[22]

Many are celebrating the Arab people's desire for freedom and democracy, but at the same time they fear that what follows may be as bad or in some cases worse than what was there before. The question everyone is asking is this: Who will fill the void? It's likely that the Arab awakening will be hijacked and exploited by murderous Islamists and jihadists who are more oppressive and dangerous than the despots they replace. In other words, don't expect the Arab Spring to be followed by a summer of love in the Middle East. Rather, the uprisings could prove to be "a Trojan Horse for radical Islam."[23]

The protests in the Middle East have presented a golden opportunity for Islamic radicals to assert themselves. For example, among Gaddafi foes in Libya, one U.S. general said he detected "flickers of al-Qaeda."[24] Those flickers could become a firestorm of terror if these foes secure power in Libya. Jihadists are certainly not letting this crisis "go to waste." *Stratfor Global Intelligence* summarizes the situation well:

> In this case, whatever the cause of the risings, there is

no question that radical Islamists will attempt to take advantage and control of them. Why wouldn't they? It is a rational and logical course for them. Whether they will be able to do so is a more complex and important question, but that they would want to and are trying to do so is obvious. They are a broad, transnational and disparate group brought up in conspiratorial methods. This is their opportunity to create a broad international coalition. Thus, as with traditional communists and the New Left in the 1960s, they did not create the rising but they would be fools not to try to take advantage of it. Democratic revolutions have two phases. The first is the establishment of democracy. The second is the election of governments. The example of Hitler is useful as a caution on what kind of governments a young democracy can produce, since he came to power through democratic and constitutional means—and then abolished democracy to cheering crowds. So there are three crosscurrents here. The first is the reaction against corrupt regimes. The second is the election itself. And the third? The United States needs to remember, as it applauds the rise of democracy, that the elected government may not be what one expected. The democracies that eventually arise will produce regimes that will take their bearings from their own culture, which means Islam. The problem with revolutions is that the people who start them rarely finish them.[25]

As bad as the current leaders in the Middle East and North Africa are, they have been reluctant to go up against Israel because they know they can't win an all-out war. They've tried before and been unsuccessful. However, the radicals who replace them would most likely not be constrained by the same fear and won't be as concerned about self-preservation as they are about destroying Israel. They won't have the imbedded dynasties and riches to protect like the current leaders have.

One example of a group that has taken advantage of the current situation is the Palestinian terrorist organization Hamas, which has long been committed to the complete destruction of Israel and has been pounding southern Israel with rockets. Recently the less-radical half of the Palestinians, Fatah, has chosen to make peace with Hamas so that their two groups are now under one leadership. The implications of this development are very serious for Israel.

Every year, when the Israelis celebrate the anniversary of the birth of the modern state of Israel, Palestinians mark the day by calling it *nakba* (catastrophe). On that day in 2011, Hamas prime minister Ismail Haniyeh spoke to Muslim worshipers, telling them to pray for an end to Israel. He said, "'Palestinians mark the *nakba* with great hope of bringing to an end the Zionist project in Palestine."[26] He told 10,000 people at Gaza City's al-Omari mosque, 'To achieve our goals in the liberation of our occupied land, we should have one leadership." He said this in recognition and praise of the recent unification of Hamas and Fatah and added that Hamas would not recognize Israel's right to exist. This uniting of forces under Hamas, joined with Hezbollah in Lebanon, could seize the current unrest as an opportune time to draw Israel into another war.

The fortunes of groups like al-Qaeda and nations like Iran

rise as the dictators of the Middle East fall or struggle to survive. It now seems clear that "in the uncertainty of dramatic changes sweeping the Middle East and North Africa, what's certain is that Israel will have fewer friends and perhaps more hostile neighbors."[27] Meir Litvak, director of the Center for Iranian Studies at Tel Aviv University, states, "A weaker Egypt in the Middle East…leaves a certain vacuum in which Iran can play a more active role, and that is not beneficial."[28] All the unrest and upheaval serves the purpose of Iran and its Shiite, mullah regime in that it dilutes and diffuses the power of Sunnis in places like Saudi Arabia, Jordan, and Egypt. In fact, Iran was on the sidelines cheering the revolt in Egypt and the fall of the house of Mubarak.

As of this writing, Egypt is susceptible to a political takeover by the Muslim Brotherhood, which is a worldwide Sunni Islamist movement now boasting chapters in about 80 nations. If the Muslim Brotherhood gains a slice of the power in Egypt, it would undoubtedly be cozy with Hamas and do all it could to undermine any kind of peace agreement with Israel. The Muslim Brotherhood has already called for a referendum on the Camp David accords with Israel.

Since its founding in 1928, the Muslim Brotherhood has been "an important incubator of Islamist movements."[29] This group is the quintessential radical Islamic organization—in fact, it gave birth to al-Qaeda. What's more, al-Qaeda's number two leader, Ayman al Zawahiri, was a high-level member of the Egyptian Muslim Brotherhood before embarking on his reign of terror, murder, and oppression with Osama bin Laden and al Qaeda. The Muslim Brotherhood has spawned several other religious and political organizations in the Middle East, including Hamas and Palestinian Islamic Jihad.

The Brotherhood is dedicated to the jihadi credo "Allah is our objective, the Quran is our Constitution, the Prophet is our leader, Jihad is our way, and death for the sake of Allah is the highest of our aspirations." The organization's charter and website state that the Muslim Brotherhood seeks to install an Islamic empire ruled under sharia law and a caliphate across the Muslim world—and ultimately the entire world—through stages designed to incrementally "Islamisize" targeted nations. Those who want this Islamic caliphate need the one key ingredient that's always required for sudden, dramatic change—chaos and unrest.

We have all the makings today of what we might call a "Recipe for Middle East Turmoil." Here are the key ingredients and instructions:

- Take one land (Israel) and try to divide it into two equal parts. Set aside one portion for the Arabs, but don't do anything with it yet.

- Add in the explosion of radical Shiite-Muslim extremism and Jewish nationalism.

- Add a pinch of Mahmoud Ahmadinejad, Bashir al-Assad, the Muslim Brotherhood, and jihadist terror.

- Add chaos and unrest that opens the doors for radical elements to gain a foothold in Egypt, Libya, and other Arab states.

- Add the possible proliferation of nuclear weapons.
- Mix well and let simmer until it explodes.[30]

In light of these recent developments, the situation for Israel has become increasingly dire. A growing number of radical Islamic leaders are threatening that Israel will soon be wiped off the map and are pledging to assist in that effort in whatever ways they can. Iran is feverishly trying to cross the nuclear "finish line" by building nuclear weapons and the ballistic missiles to deliver them. In Lebanon, Hezbollah has stockpiled a supply of more than 40,000 rockets aimed at Israel. Syria has spent billions on weapons systems targeting Israel, and with the rise of the Muslim Brotherhood in Egypt, Egyptian leaders are speaking with growing hostility toward the Jewish State.

To make matters worse, if that's possible, at the same time the Middle East is burning, President Obama has called for Israel to return to its 1967 borders as a basis for the creation of the neighboring Palestinian State. Israel's number one and most powerful ally is putting Israel in a no-win situation, or "throwing them under the bus," as some have put it. Obama's plan would mean the Palestinians would control the Gaza Strip, the West Bank, and East Jerusalem.

Israeli prime minister Benjamin Netanyahu immediately rejected the notion of a return to the 1967 borders. He said, "Remember that before 1967, Israel was all of nine miles wide. It was half the width of the Washington Beltway. And these were not the boundaries of peace; they were the boundaries of repeated wars, because the attack on Israel was so attractive."[31] President Obama's statements about Israel highlight the fact that the deep, smoldering issue for the Arabs is still the Israeli-Palestinian issue. Obama knows that this issue must be resolved, but his answer is historically shortsighted, politically unpopular, and biblically reckless. In light of these latest developments, many orthodox Jewish rabbis and a growing number of Christians believe that the Middle East could explode at any time into a major regional conflagration.

And in fact, there are signs that we're headed in that direction. The Institute of International Finance predicted that economic growth in Egypt, Jordan, Morocco, and Syria will fall dramatically in the near future. It is increasingly difficult to carry out normal business, crime is soaring, and the political future is profoundly uncertain. Rich Arabs are pulling their money out fast. They don't trust the Arab revolution. "Since January [2011] they have been rushing to get their cash into safe havens, some arriving in London or Zurich with suitcases full of cash."[32]

There are estimates that as much as $30 billion has fled from Egypt alone since the outbreak of the Arab Spring. The Egyptian stock market is tanking, having plunged 23 percent from its peak before the crisis. Foreign investors don't want anything to do with the region. The unsettling bottom line is that economic conditions have gotten far worse, not better, since the onset of the Arab Spring. Unemployment is rising in Egypt and inflation has increased 12 percent. Many of the same conditions that precipitated the Arab uprising—high unemployment, high food prices, and corruption—have increased, while living standards are declining. This is the perfect setup for extremists like the Muslim Brotherhood and al-Qaeda to come in and "peddle their radical ideology of war against internal and external foes."[33] If things don't begin to improve quickly, horrific civil war could erupt between the forces of revolution and reaction.

Foreshadows of the Future

Those who know the Bible recognize that Scripture tells us the Middle East will be the staging ground for the great wars of the end times, including the Battle of Gog and Magog as well as the mother of all wars, Armageddon. So their eyes are riveted on the Middle East, and they are acutely aware of the significance of any developments that have the potential to lead the Middle East closer to these cataclysmic events.

Almost 30 years ago, Bible prophecy scholar John Walvoord noted that the first key to the Armageddon countdown is that "the Middle East must become the number one crisis in the world."[34] After this he added, "Then as nations jockey to gain influence and control, a new world order will begin to emerge. This sets the stage for the emergence of a new ten-nation group that will superimpose a peaceful solution in a seemingly impossible situation."[35] There's no doubt today that the Middle East is the number one crisis spot in the world. That piece of the prophetic puzzle is now firmly in place. There's also no doubt that everyone recognizes the need for a comprehensive peace plan for the Middle East.

In 1967, Dr. John Walvoord wrote some timely words that look like they were taken straight from today's headlines. What he says here is clearly more applicable today than when he wrote it almost 45 years ago:

The world today faces an international crisis unparalleled in all the history of man. A tremendous revolution is under way in the international scene, in science, in economics, in morals, in theology, and in the religious structure of the church. The world is aflame with the raw passions of men ambitious for power and desperate to be freed from poverty and frustration. An ominous cloud hangs over the hearts of men and nations. The nations are indeed at the crossroads, and impending events cast their shadow on every aspect of human life. The world is moving faster and faster like a colossal machine out of control whose very power and momentum inevitably will plunge it into ultimate disaster.

Apart from the Bible, the world does not have a ray of hope. Our most brilliant leaders have not found an answer. World leaders, whether in Moscow or Washington, are troubled by the great issues which face the world today…

The present world crisis is not a result of any one factor, but a concurrence of causes and effects which combine to set the world stage for a conflict which may quickly bring an end to hundreds of years of progress in western civilization and establish new centers of international power. Whatever the future holds, it is going to be dramatically different than the past. In this dark picture only the Scriptures chart a sure course and give us an intelligent explanation of worldwide confusion as it exists today. The present world crisis in the light of the Scriptures reveals the existence of remarkable components in almost every area which may lead to a dramatic climax of world history. The present crisis in every area of human life all point to the same conclusion, that disaster awaits the nations of the world.[36]

How Much Longer Can the Lid Be Held Down?

The rapidly increasing tempo of change in modern life and the constant upheavals and uncertainty in global hot spots has given the entire world a sense of impending crisis. The entire Middle East became the center of attention during the Gulf War in 1990–1991 and made many wonder whether that conflict was the final war predicted in Scripture. Although it soon became clear that the Gulf War was not a fulfillment of biblical prophecy, the entire world has kept its eyes intently focused on the Middle East ever since.

The invasions of Afghanistan in 2001 and Iraq in 2003 seem to have added fuel to the jihadist fire. Israel fought a 34-day war with Hamas and Hezbollah in the summer of 2006. The spring of 2011 brought a series of revolutions to the Middle East and North Africa that are still smoldering. Iran is in hot pursuit of nuclear weapons and could be planning nuclear jihad against Israel. Israel is equipped to unleash a preemptive strike against Iran's nuclear facilities. Given all these factors, how much longer can world tensions be kept in check? How much longer can Western powers keep their struggle with Islamic jihadists from becoming a global bloodbath?

People everywhere are asking questions about the future as never before—sober questions that have serious implications:

- Are biblical prophecies being fulfilled before our eyes?

- How do the enormous changes taking place now in the Middle East fit into God's prophetic puzzle?

- Will some of the Arab nations now experiencing unrest eventually join the Islamic jihad and turn against Israel even more aggressively?

- Could the Arab Spring turn into a nuclear winter?

- How do Egypt, Jordan, Libya, Iran, Syria, Russia, and Turkey fit into God's prophetic program?

- What will happen to Israel?

- What does the Bible say about coming wars in the Middle East?

- Where, if anywhere, does the United States fit in all this?

The Middle East is burning. That much is clear. But what does it all mean? What will happen next? Where is all this headed? The Bible is certainly the best place to look for answers. Many of the biblical prophecies cited in this book are strikingly foreshadowed by events happening right before our eyes. People everywhere are becoming increasingly aware of an astonishing correspondence between the obvious trend of world events and what the Bible predicted centuries ago.

In fact, 28 percent of the Bible was prophetic at the time it was written. Even the most skeptical person can put these prophecies to the test by noting the literal, precise fulfillment of hundreds of biblical prophecies that have already come to pass. When it comes to prophecy, the Bible has a proven track record of 100 percent accuracy. For this reason, biblical prophecy is being discussed more than ever before. Prophecies that, in the past, were sometimes brushed aside as being too far-fetched or impossible are now being studied again. People of all walks of life and of all religious faiths are asking the burning question: What does the Bible say the future holds?

Chapter 2

What's Next?

Do not seal up the words of the prophecy
of this book, for the time is near.

REVELATION 22:10

Our planet is awash in uncertainty. It's being pounded by relentless waves of instability. Financial volatility. Moral shift. Political unrest. Lack of confidence in government. Revolution. Concern that new Middle East "democracies" will turn against Israel and trigger a regional or global war. Worries about disruption of oil supplies. Earthquakes and tsunamis are literally shaking the ground beneath us and surging the waters around us.

As a result, nations and people are being shaken to the core. Fear of the future is mounting. People everywhere are wondering, What does all of this mean? Are we seeing the beginning of the end? Are we experiencing the birth pains Jesus talked about in Matthew 24:8? What does all this portend for the future? Are there any answers?

Given the world scenario right now, it's not surprising that polls indicate Americans have an increased interest in a better

understanding of Bible prophecy and future events. A Pew
Research poll found that

- 72 percent of Americans anticipate a major world
  energy crisis
- 58 percent see another world war as "definite or
  probable"
- 41 percent believe Jesus Christ will return by the
  year 2050
- 59 percent believe the prophecies of the book of
  Revelation will come to pass[1]

Other similar polls have revealed that

- 55 percent of Americans believe "that before the
  world ends the religiously faithful will be saved"
- 46 percent of Americans agree "the world will end
  in the Battle of Armageddon between Jesus and
  the Antichrist"[2]

As alarming as events are today, they are not at all surprising in light of the Bible's end-times prophecies. For centuries, Christians have considered the message of the true prophets in Scripture to be God's revelation of His plan for human history. The Old Testament records the lives and works of many of these prophets—Moses, Isaiah, Jeremiah, Ezekiel, Daniel, Joel, Micah, Zechariah, and others. These men predicted future events in vivid detail, including the rise and fall of every major world empire that would leave its imprint on the Middle East. Some of their predictions came true within their lifetimes, while others were fulfilled later. Today it appears that the groundwork has been laid for a particularly crucial set of prophecies that have not yet been fulfilled—those that have to do with the last days of planet Earth.

Unlike the self-proclaimed prophets of today or alleged seers of days gone by like Nostradamus, Jesus and the biblical prophets did not peddle vague, general predictions that could be adjusted and manipulated to fit almost any situation. The prophecies recorded in the Bible are stunningly specific, detailed, and intricately interwoven. Although people continue to disagree on the interpretation of minor, secondary points, the overall picture regarding the end times is disturbingly clear. The world is headed for a time of unparalleled trouble and confusion that will culminate in a great final death struggle in the Middle East known as Armageddon. And the Bible also mentions a whole series of carefully timed events that will serve as signposts that indicate we're on the road to Armageddon. These events will precede and lay the groundwork for the last great conflict.

According to the Bible, the final countdown to the end of the age will span a period of years, not months or days. And even before that countdown begins, a number of preparatory events, which are predicted in the Bible, will shape the political, economic, and religious landscape necessary for end-time events to unfold. These preliminary moves now appear to be falling into place in rapid succession in many places, especially the Middle East. As these stage-setting moves are completed, a more specific timetable of events will begin to emerge, with a period of seven years clearly delineated in Scripture as a unique time of tribulation and judgment. These final seven years are often referred to as the tribulation period. The last half of these seven years will see three-and-a-half years of unparalleled disaster and war and are often called the Great Tribulation, which will climax at the final great battle known as Armageddon.

Major Events to Watch For

We will examine some of these events in greater detail as we continue through this book. But for now, let's take a brief glimpse at the major happenings that will lead up to and include the end times. This will help us get our bearings with regard to where we stand today and what we can expect in the future—possibly very soon.

Event #1: The Regathering

The most prophesied event in end-time passages in the Bible is the return of the Jewish people to their promised land. The Bible predicts over and over again that the Jews must be back in their homeland before the events of the end times can unfold (see Jeremiah 30:1-3; Ezekiel 34:11-24; Ezekiel 37; Zechariah 10:6-10). Almost all the key events of the end times hinge in one way or another on the existence of the nation of Israel. Israel is the battleground for all the great end-time wars and conflicts described in the Bible, and the end times will officially begin when the Antichrist makes a seven-year treaty with Israel (Daniel 9:27). Also, in Ezekiel 38 and Zechariah 12 we read about armed invasions of the nation of Israel. Obviously, for any of these things to happen, the Jewish people must be back in their land.

Scripture indicates that this regathering of Israel will occur in stages. It is portrayed as a process. In the famous "valley of dry bones" vision of Ezekiel 37:1-14, the bones symbolize the nation of Israel coming back together in the end times. In that passage, Ezekiel sees a graveyard of bones that come to life, illustrating the national return, restoration, and regeneration of "the whole house of Israel" (37:11). At first this restoration is physical in nature—this is pictured in Ezekiel 37 by the coming together of bones and sinew. The complete skeleton will come together piece by piece, bone by bone. But at this point the body is still a lifeless corpse (37:8).

Then Ezekiel witnesses Israel's spiritual regeneration, which occurs when the breath of the Spirit breathes life into the dead nation (37:9). Of course, this spiritual regeneration won't occur until the Messiah returns. But the process of physical regathering to the land has been going on now for about 130 years. A pile of bones has been coming together and taking shape in the land of Israel.

The modern beginning of the return to the land began as early as 1871, when a few Jews began to trickle back into the land. By 1881, about 25,000 Jews had settled there. At the first Zionist congress in 1897, led by Theodor Herzl, the goal of reclaiming the land for the Jewish people was officially adopted. During the first few decades, the regathering was very slow. By 1914, the number of Jews in the land was only 80,000.

During World War I, the British sought support from the Jews for the war effort. So the British foreign secretary, Arthur J. Balfour, issued what became known as the Balfour Declaration on November 2, 1917. The declaration was stated in a letter from Balfour to Lord Rothschild, a wealthy Jewish entrepreneur. In the letter, Secretary Balfour expressed Britain's approval of the Jewish people's goal of reclaiming their ancient land. "His Majesty's Government views with favor the establishment in Palestine of a national home for the Jewish people..." But due to Arab pressure and Britain's desire to maintain friendly relations with the Arabs, little was done to act upon the Balfour Declaration. Nevertheless, this declaration stirred Jewish hopes for the establishment of a homeland in the Holy Land and encouraged more Jews to return. By 1939, when World War II broke out, about 450,000 Jews had managed to return to their homeland.

The Second World War and Nazi Germany's heinous, despicable treatment of the Jewish people created a worldwide sympathy and favorable environment for the Jewish people. Hitler's atrocities actually ended up providing great momentum for the establishment of a national homeland for the Jews. The United Nations gave its approval for this homeland, and British control over the Holy Land ended on May 14, 1948. The new nation was given 5000 square miles of territory, which by this time was populated by 650,000 Jews and several hundred thousand Arabs. Further waves of immigrants continued to pour into Israel from all over the world, most notably from Ethiopia and the Soviet Union.

In 2009, for the first time since AD 135, there are now more Jews in Israel than in any other place on earth. There are now 5.4 million Jews there, compared to 5.2 million in the United States, according to the latest United Jewish Appeal Federation survey.[3] According to Haaretz.com, "The data indicates the closure of a historical circle: For the first time since the destruction of the Second Temple, Israel has once again become the largest concentration of Jews in the world."[4] To put this in perspective, in 1948 only 6 percent of the Jews in the world were in Israel. Today, that figure stands at almost 40 percent. By the year 2030 it is estimated that half of the Jews worldwide will be back in the land.

From a prophetic standpoint, the process of regathering that has taken place over the last 130 years is staggering. For the first time in 2000 years, the Jews have returned and continue to come home to their land, just as the ancient prophets predicted. This stands as a significant affirmation that we can trust what the Bible says about the future.

Of special interest is that fact that every foreign visitor to modern Israel who enters by plane comes in the same way: through the passport control area at the Ben Gurion airport in Tel Aviv. Upon exiting that area, you are greeted by a huge and colorful tapestry welcoming you to the land. Millions of people have come and gone through that airport, but most probably never even notice this big welcome sign.

On this tapestry is depicted masses of people streaming into the gates of the city of Jerusalem. On it, in Hebrew, is a prophetic text from the book of Jeremiah that speaks about the ingathering of the exiles: "'So there is hope for your future,' declares the Lord. 'Your children will return to their own land'" (Jeremiah 31:17 NIV). Whether or not the incoming Jewish people can read the words, the lesson is understood: Those who are coming home are part of God's present plan to regather His people in the fulfillment of His ancient promise.[5]

The number one sign of the times, and the greatest miracle of the twentieth century, is the return of the Jewish people to their homeland from worldwide exile. And we are the generation that has a front row seat at the time when this is happening. We are witnessing what those in former generations only dreamed of. And this one fulfillment points toward the fulfillment of other key end-time prophecies.

Now consider this ingathering in the context of Israel being the focal point of world news today. One is hard-pressed to open a newspaper or listen to a newscast without some mention of Israel. The wave of revolt in the Middle East is occurring in the nations that surround Israel, and for many of those nations, relations with Israel are at the heart of the unrest. Israel is at the center of attention, just as the Bible predicted. Israel is the fuse for the powder keg of the final world conflict. Nothing can happen until Israel is back in her land; it all hangs on Israel. The Tribulation can't start until Israel is back in the land and willing to make peace with the Antichrist as prophesied in Daniel 9:27. For the first time in almost 2000 years, the fuse is moving into place. Israel has been reborn as a nation. Millions of Jews are back in the land. As this and other prophetic signposts line up, we can know that the world is making its way toward Armageddon and the coming of the Lord may be very near.

Event #2: The Rapture

One stormy night not long ago, my son's car was broken into in our driveway. The thieves broke a window and got away with an iPod and some speakers. The next morning when I saw the damage, I was instantly reminded that Jesus had told His followers that He will one day come back like a thief in the night. I was also reminded that thieves come unannounced, suddenly, and stealthily. No one knows the time of their arrival. Yet, in spite of Jesus' clear statements to this effect, many people have foolishly attempted to set dates for the coming of the Lord only to be proven wrong every time. These reckless date setters give Christianity a black eye and provide cannon fodder for those who enjoy mocking the idea of the Lord's coming, but no matter how loud the ridicule of the rapture becomes, its reality cannot be smothered.

Someday, any day, perhaps soon, the world will be traumatized suddenly and unexpectedly by the fulfillment of the rapture of the church—the sudden removal of every Christian from the earth. This event, which will change the world forever in an instant of time, is vividly prophesied in 1 Thessalonians 4:13-18:

> We do not want you to be uninformed, brethren, about those who are asleep, so that you will not grieve as do the rest who have no hope. For if we believe that Jesus died and rose again, even so God will bring with Him those who have fallen asleep in Jesus. For this we say to you by the word of the Lord, that we who are alive and remain until the coming of the Lord, will not precede those who have fallen asleep. For the Lord Himself will descend from heaven with a shout, with the voice of the archangel and with the trumpet of God, and the dead in Christ will rise first. Then we who are alive and remain will be caught up together with them in the clouds to meet the Lord in the air,

and so we shall always be with the Lord. Therefore comfort one another with these words.

This stunning event will fulfill the reassuring promise of Christ to His disciples on the night before He died, when He said, "I will come again and receive you to Myself, that where I am, there you may be also" (John 14:3). At that time, the bodies of Christians who have died will be resurrected and rejoined with their perfected spirits, and every Christian alive on the earth will suddenly be removed to heaven without experiencing death. They will do an end-run on the grave.

The rapture is the next great event on God's prophetic calendar, and it could happen any day. Scripturally, there's nothing that must occur before the rapture can take place. There are no signs that must precede it. It can happen at any time. Needless to say, the rapture will shock the world. Imagine the simultaneous, instantaneous disappearance of millions of people all over the globe. For half the world, this will take place at night. Beds will be emptied, or one will be taken and one left behind. For the other half of the world, there will be unimaginable chaos: cars without drivers, airplanes without pilots, people from all walks of life will suddenly vanish without a trace, leaving a pile of clothes with watches, jewelry, glasses, and even dentures for some. The disappearance of millions of Christians will deepen the religious, political, and economic mayhem already present in the world, paving the way for power to fall into the hands of religious, economic, and political opportunists who are waiting in the wings.

Event #3: The Reuniting of the Roman Empire

In the chaos that will inevitably follow the rapture, people will desperately look for answers, for someone who can bring some order out of the maelstrom. The Bible teaches that a group of ten leaders, or what we might call the Group of Ten, will rise from Europe. These ten leaders are symbolized by the ten toes of Nebuchadnezzar's image in Daniel 2:41-44, the ten horns of the dreadful beast in Daniel 7:8, and the similar description of the end-time government in Revelation 13:1.

This alliance or confederacy of ten leaders and the nations they represent will constitute a revival or reuniting of the Roman Empire and will herald the beginning of the final stage of the fourth beast described in Daniel 7. The Group of Ten will evidently rise to power because the West will desperately need to guarantee the peace and security of the Middle East and possibly the continued supply of oil. This will temporarily be accomplished with the help of a seven-year covenant of peace and protection with Israel. Without this forced peace, chaos, disruption of the West's oil supply, and an escalation in terrorism will threaten to bring Western civilization to its knees. Within the 27 nations that currently comprise the European Union we see what almost certainly is the embryonic stage of this final world power.

Event #4: The Coming Middle East Peace

The date for the rebirth of Israel as a nation was Friday, May 14, 1948. But the nation's birth was not without serious complications. Israel was surrounded by seven nations that vehemently opposed the establishment of the Jewish State. From the moment of her birth, Israel has remained in a state of war with most of her Arab neighbors (except for Egypt and Jordan, but that may be about to change). Israel's neighbors refuse to even acknowledge her existence. The Middle East peace process began days before Israel became a nation when Golda Meir, who later became prime minister, made a secret journey to Amman, Jordan. She visited King Abdullah, dressing like an Arab and placing a veil over her face. The purpose of her visit was to forge a peaceful agreement between Israel and Jordan. They both wanted peace, but King Abdullah was trapped by the furor for war that had gripped the Arab masses. As Golda Meir departed, the king's last words were, "I am sorry. I deplore the coming bloodshed and destruction. Let us hope we shall meet again and not sever relations."[6] They never saw each other again.

Golda Meir was the first leader in modern times to try to bring peace between Israel and the Arabs, and she certainly is not the last. One US secretary of state after another has tried in vain to solve the Middle East crisis. Egyptian president Anwar Sadat made a historic trip to Jerusalem in 1977 for face-to-face talks with Israeli prime minister Menachem Begin, raising hopes for a final, lasting peace. A follow-up meeting between the two men with President Jimmy Carter at Camp David in Maryland produced the Camp David Accord on September 17, 1978. The agreement was formally ratified on April 25, 1979. Egypt became the first Arab nation to recognize Israel's right to exist as a nation.

The Gulf War in 1991 resurrected the peace process and Secretary of State James Baker arranged the first face-to-face meeting between Israel and her neighbors since 1948. In another milestone in the marathon pursuit of peace, on September 13, 1993, PLO leader Yasser Arafat and Israeli prime minister Yitzhak Rabin shook hands on the White House lawn with Bill Clinton after signing the Oslo Accords.

Further attempts at peace in the Middle East have failed miserably. People everywhere wonder if there will ever be peace in that part of the world. Incredibly, the Bible predicts a coming temporary peace that will come upon the world, including the Middle East, as a prelude to end-time events. This brief period of peace is described by the apostle Paul in 1 Thessalonians 5:1-3:

> Now as to the times and the epochs, brethren, you have no need of anything to be written to you. For you yourselves know full well that the day of the Lord will come just like a thief in the night. While they are saying, "Peace and safety!" then destruction will come upon them suddenly like labor pains upon a woman with child, and they will not escape.

According to Scripture, the terrible time of coming tribulation will catch the world totally off guard. The world will be basking in the sunlight of peace, albeit temporary. This portrait of peace, especially in the Middle East, seems so remote and unimaginable today. How will Israel ever reach a point when it feels secure? Daniel 9:27 provides the likely answer: "He will make a firm covenant with the many for one week, but in the middle of the week he will put a stop to sacrifice and grain offering; and on the wing of abominations will come one who makes desolate, even until a complete destruction, one that is decreed, is poured out on the one who makes desolate."

The nearest antecedent for the "he" in verse 27 is the "prince who is to come" in verse 26. This person is the coming world ruler or final Antichrist, who will rise alongside a group of ten world leaders and then splash onto the world stage by forging a peace agreement between Israel and her neighbors. From the host of negotiators and leaders involved in the Middle East one new international leader will emerge (a person of European descent) to superimpose a peace settlement on Israel and the more militant Muslims and put an end to the chaos in the Middle East and likely assure the West's supply of oil. Daniel 9:27 tells us that the signing of this treaty will commence the final seven years of this age, or the seven-year Tribulation.

Revelation 6:1-2 also describes this coming peace: "Then I saw when the Lamb broke one of the seven seals, and I heard one of the four living creatures saying as with a voice of thunder, 'Come.' I looked, and behold, a white horse, and he who sat on it had a bow; and a crown was given to him, and he went out conquering and to conquer." The rider on this white horse is a false, counterfeit Messiah—the Antichrist—who will enter the global scene as a great peacemaker. This move will usher in an era of false peace, a move toward disarmament, and a major push for a new world economic system.

All of this is foreshadowed by what we see taking place around us today. The only real hope for the Middle East is some kind of strong, enforceable, comprehensive, imposed peace initiative. And the rest of the world is crying out for peace as well. The attainment of peace in the Middle East is the number one foreign policy and diplomatic issue of our day, and the Bible predicted a coming temporary peace—both in Israel and worldwide—some 2500 years ago.

Event #5: Israel Is Attacked

As Israel lets down her guard for the first time in modern history on account of the peace treaty prophesied in Daniel 9:27, the nations that surround her, including Russia and Iran, will see her vulnerability and will devise a plan to storm her and, at the same time, deal a decisive blow against the Western leader who brokered the seven-year peace treaty (Ezekiel 38–39). This will usher in the Battle of Gog and Magog. Moved by hatred for Israel and jealousy over her abundant prosperity, the strike force will come like a storm at the appointed time. We will look at this event, and how today's headlines point toward its fulfillment, in detail in chapters 4–7.

Event #6: Power Centralized in One Man

During the last three-and-a-half years of the Tribulation the world will experience a series of almost inconceivable catastrophes, which are outlined in Revelation chapters 8–18. Just before this period begins, Russia and a group of Islamic allies will attempt a final power grab in the Middle East, but their armies will be supernaturally destroyed (Ezekiel 38–39). As you can imagine, this event will dramatically reshape world geopolitics. The balance of power will swing decisively to the world's new strongman, the Antichrist. As Satan's man of the hour, he will seize the opportunity and attempt to destroy Israel, now disarmed and at peace. In the same manner as the Babylonian and Roman emperors of ancient times, he will deify himself and command the worship of the world (2 Thessalonians 2:4). This final period of three-and-a-half years will be the time Jesus spoke of as the "great tribulation" (Matthew 24:21).

Event #7: The March to Armageddon

Climaxing all these future events will be a world war of unprecedented proportions. Hundreds of millions of troops will be involved in a gigantic world power struggle centered in the land of Israel at a place called Armageddon (Revelation 16:13-16). The term *Armageddon*, in our popular culture, is greatly overused and misunderstood. It has come to describe anyone's worst fear or any great catastrophe. But in Scripture, the prophets specifically spoke of Armageddon in reference to the final worldwide struggle centered in the Middle East. It will be the final act after a terrifying series of events that are very much related to today's headlines. This history-ending war will occur in the exact location and at the specific time predicted in Scripture.

The name *Armageddon* comes from a Hebrew word meaning "the Mount of Megiddo," which is a small mountain located in northern Israel at the end of a broad valley. This valley, which is 14 miles wide and 20 miles long, has been the scene of many military conflicts in the past and will be the location of history's greatest war. Massive armies from all over the world will pour into Israel for this final death struggle, and millions will perish. That is what Armageddon is all about.

Event #8: The Second Coming of Christ

As the world's military powers are engaged in battle at Armageddon, Jesus Christ will come back in power and glory from heaven. His coming, accompanied by millions of angels and raptured Christians, is graphically described in Revelation 19:11-21:

> I saw heaven opened, and behold, a white horse, and He who sat on it is called Faithful and True, and in righteousness He judges and wages war. His eyes are a flame of fire, and on His head are many diadems; and He has a name written on Him which no one knows except Himself. He is clothed with a robe dipped in blood, and His name is called The Word of God. And the armies which are in heaven, clothed in fine linen, white and clean, were following Him on white horses. From His mouth comes a sharp sword, so that with it He may strike down the nations, and He will rule them with a rod of iron; and He treads the wine press of the fierce wrath of God, the Almighty. And on His robe and on His thigh He has a name written, "KING OF KINGS, AND LORD OF LORDS."
>
> Then I saw an angel standing in the sun, and he cried out with a loud voice, saying to all the birds which fly in midheaven, "Come, assemble for the great supper of God, so that you may eat the flesh of kings and the flesh of commanders and the flesh of mighty men and the flesh of horses and of those who sit on them and the flesh of all men, both free men and slaves, and small and great."
>
> And I saw the beast and the kings of the earth and their armies assembled to make war against Him who sat on the horse and against His army. And the beast was

seized, and with him the false prophet who performed the signs in his presence, by which he deceived those who had received the mark of the beast and those who worshiped his image; these two were thrown alive into the lake of fire which burns with brimstone. And the rest were killed with the sword which came from the mouth of Him who sat on the horse, and all the birds were filled with their flesh.

Coming as the King of kings and judge of the world, Jesus will destroy the contending armies and usher in His own 1000-year kingdom of peace and righteousness on earth, also known as the millennium (Revelation 20:1-6).

Everything Is in Place

As incredible as these prophecies are, even now the world stage is being set. People everywhere seem to have the foreboding sense that something ominous is on the horizon. The whole world is focused upon the Middle East, which the Bible said would be the case in the end. Israel is a powerful nation surrounded by a sea of enemies. The desperate cry for peace in the Middle East is unrelenting. The nations of the Roman Empire are reforming. Dramatic changes in the Arab nations point toward an all-out war with Israel. Globalism makes the rule of one man over the entire earth possible for the first time in human history.

All the necessary preparatory elements are falling into place. The signposts are lining up. The groundwork is being laid. Like pieces on a chessboard or actors on a set, the nations are moving into place for the final act. The prophecies about the last days—which were uttered some 2000 years ago—will be fulfilled just as literally as the prophecies that came to pass long ago. The world will rush headlong to the destiny set forth in the pages of Scripture.

Chapter 3

The Four Power
Blocs of the Future

*Russia is poised to the north of the Holy Land for entry in
the end-time conflict. Egypt and other African countries
have not abandoned their desire to attack Israel from
the south. Red China in the east is now a military power
great enough to field an army as large as that described
in the book of Revelation. Each nation is prepared to
play out its role in the final hours of history. Our present
world is well prepared for the beginning of the prophetic
drama that will lead to Armageddon. Since the stage
is set for this dramatic climax of the age, it must mean
that Christ's coming for His own is very near. If there ever
was an hour when men should consider their personal
relationship to Jesus Christ, it is today. God is saying to
this generation: "Prepare for the coming of the Lord."*[1]

JOHN F. WALVOORD, *ARMAGEDDON,
OIL AND THE MIDDLE EAST CRISIS* (1974)

I like the story of the man who visited his psychic and saw a
sign on the door that said, "Closed due to unforeseen circumstances." Man's resume is pretty thin when it comes to
accurately predicting the future. Only the Word of God has
answers about what is to come. There are no unforeseen circumstances with God. There is never panic in heaven. The

Trinity never meets in an emergency session. God knows the end from the beginning. If we are to know anything about the future, we have to turn to the pages of Scripture and see what the prophets said.

The Picture on the Box

What's the key to successfully putting a jigsaw puzzle together? The picture on the box. Likewise, God's prophecies in the Bible serve as the guide, master plan, or picture on the box by which we can evaluate the many current events in our world today to see how they fit together in God's program for this world.

One key part of the picture on the box is the end-time alignment of nations we find presented in Scripture. During the seven-year Tribulation, the world will be divided into four main power blocs or spheres of political influence. The alignments of these four blocs will rise and fall at different times, and if we're going to accurately understand what's going on in the world today and what lies ahead, especially for the Middle East, we need to understand the basic framework of these end-time power blocs.

We Four Kings

As we look around us today, we can already see the foreshadows of the four end-time power blocs described in Scripture:

The king of the West	The Western confederacy of the Antichrist
The king of the North	The Russian-Iranian-Turkish alliance

The kings of the East	The Far Eastern federation
The king of the South	The North African coalition

The geographical directions mentioned in connection with each of these powers is given in relation to Israel, which, from God's perspective, is "the center of the world" (Ezekiel 38:12).

Obviously, not every nation on the earth during the end times will be part of one of these blocs, but generally speaking, these four blocs will comprise the geopolitical players of the end times. Let's begin our examination of what the Bible says about the future of the Middle East—and the world—by understanding these four key global powers.

The King of the West

While the Antichrist is never specifically called the king of the West, this title is an apt description of the final world ruler since, according to Scripture, he will dominate the Western confederacy that will comprise a revived or reunited Roman Empire. He will initially be the leader of the West and will ultimately expand his empire to include the entire world during the final three-and-a-half years of the Tribulation (Revelation 13:4-8).

What do we know about this Western leader and his end-time coalition?

1. He will be a Gentile, not a Jew.

   Four main points support this identification: First, he will lead the final form of Gentile world power; second, he will rise from the "sea" of the nations (Revelation 13:1); third, the Old Testament type of the Antichrist was Antiochus Epiphanes, who was a Gentile (Daniel 8); and fourth, he will mercilessly persecute the Jewish people, which he wouldn't do if he were a Jew.

2. He will emerge initially as a great peacemaker (Daniel 9:27; Revelation 6:1-2).

3. In one of the great double-crosses of all time, he will break his seven-year treaty with Israel at its midpoint (Daniel 9:27) and Israel will be invaded by the nations (Ezekiel 38–39).

4. He will mercilessly persecute the Jewish people (Daniel 7:25).

5. He has many names and titles or aliases:

   The little horn (Daniel 7:8)

   A king, insolent and skilled in intrigue (Daniel 8:23)

   The prince who is to come (Daniel 9:26)

   The one who makes desolate (Daniel 9:27)

   The king who does as he pleases (Daniel 11:36-45)

   A foolish shepherd (Zechariah 11:15-17)

   The man of destruction (2 Thessalonians 2:3)

   The lawless one (2 Thessalonians 2:8)

   The rider on the white horse (Revelation 6:2)

   The beast out of the sea (Revelation 13:1-2)

These titles leave little to the imagination. The final world ruler will be the satanic superman who will rule the world.

6. He will not be a Muslim or the Islamic Mahdi.

The only passage of Scripture I know of that gives insight into the religious background of the Antichrist is found in Daniel 11:36-39. Describing the final world ruler as "the king [who] will do as he pleases," Daniel said,

> He will exalt and magnify himself above every other god…He will show no regard for the gods of his fathers or for the desire of women, nor will he show regard for any other god; for he will magnify himself above them all. But instead he will honor a god of fortresses, a god whom his fathers did not know; he will honor him with gold, silver, costly stones and treasures. He will take action against the strongest of fortresses with the help of a foreign god.

While I would agree that there are some interesting parallels between the biblical Antichrist and the Islamic Mahdi, for me this passage precludes the Islamic Antichrist view. Daniel said that the Antichrist will exalt himself above every god and will honor a god that his fathers did not know. The Antichrist could be someone who was a Muslim at some point in his life, but this means by the time he comes to power he must have rejected Allah and turned to another god—the god of fortresses or military might, and ultimately, himself. So, if he is a Muslim at some point in his life, which is possible, this passage makes clear that when he comes to power he will have turned his back on all religions and established himself as god.

Second Thessalonians 2:4 makes it clear that the Antichrist will declare that he is god. No practicing Muslim could ever do this. Certainly the Islamic Mahdi could never do this. This would violate the central tenet of Islam that there is one God, who is Allah. If the Antichrist declared himself god, he would no longer be a follower of Islam.

7. He will defile the rebuilt Jewish temple in Jerusalem (Matthew 24:15; 2 Thessalonians 2:4; Revelation 11:1-2).

8. He will declare himself to be God and demand worship (Daniel 11:37; 2 Thessalonians 2:4; Revelation 13:4,12).

9. He will have a henchman called the false prophet, who will do his bidding, perform great miracles and signs, construct an image in his honor that will breathe and speak, and point people to him as their god (Revelation 13:11-15).

10. Through the false prophet, he will institute the use of a mark that serves as a sign of allegiance to him and as a passport for people to engage in any form of commerce (Revelation 13:16-18).

The King of the North

The last days' king of the North is graphically presented in Ezekiel 38–39 and Daniel 11:40. I believe this is a northern coalition of nations led by Russia. In Daniel 11:5-35 the historical king of the North was the leader of the ancient Seleucid Empire centered in Syria; however, it included a vast territory north and east of Israel. The prophetic counterpart to the ancient Seleucid king is what we might call the prophetic king of the North. In Daniel 11:40, this seems to be great northern confederacy headed by Russia (see also Ezekiel 38–39). I view Ezekiel 38–39 and Daniel 11:40 as parallel passages describing the same invasion. We will examine Ezekiel 38–39 and the king of the North in much more detail in chapter 7.

The Kings of the East

The kings of the East are mentioned only once in Scripture, in Revelation 16:12: "The sixth angel poured out his bowl on the great river, the Euphrates; and its water was dried up, so that the way would be prepared for the kings from the east." While the kings of the East are not part of our main discussion and consideration in this book, I want to mention this power bloc so you will have a full-orbed understanding of the world powers that are present during the end times.

The precise nations that comprise this coalition are not enumerated, and the details we are given are not all that clear. But the most reasonable explanation of this prophecy, related as it is to the Euphrates River, which forms the eastern boundary of the ancient Roman Empire, is that the army comes from the Far East and crosses the Euphrates River to participate in the struggle that is taking place in the land of Israel. It is for this reason that the Euphrates River will be dried up—so that the nations in this power bloc from Far East can make their way into the Middle East. Revelation 16:14 states this movement will be part of a gathering of "the kings of the whole world… for the war of the great day of God, the Almighty." According to Revelation 16:16, the geographical focal point of this gathering is Armageddon.

The simplest and most suitable explanation for understanding "the kings from the east" (Revelation 16:12) is to take the passage literally. The kings of the East are kings from the East or "of the sun rising"—that is, they are monarchs who originate from the Far East.

All that we know about these nations, then, is that they come from east of the Euphrates River to gather at Armageddon for the final great conflict of the ages. The kings of the East probably include the nations of the Far East, such as China and Korea.

Some have pointed to the army of 200 million in Revelation 9:16 and note that China now has the capability of fielding an army of that size. If that's what John had in mind, it's incredible to think that 200 million was probably the population of the entire world in his day. While I understand the army of 200 million in Revelation 9:16 to be a demonic army unleashed in the end times, still, the size of the Chinese army today is staggering.

If what Revelation 16:12 says about the kings of the East is taken literally, it provides an important piece of information concerning the final world conflict. According to this verse, the invasion from the east starts by an act of God—He will dry up the Euphrates River. This miraculous drying up of the river will provide the tremendous army of the East with an easy passageway toward the Middle East. This act of God will allow the army to cross the dry riverbed just as the children of Israel were able to walk on dry land when they crossed the Red Sea and the Jordan River.

From the standpoint of Scripture, the Euphrates is one of the important rivers of the world. The first reference to it is found in Genesis 2:10-14, where it is mentioned as one of the four rivers having its source in the Garden of Eden. The Euphrates River is mentioned a total of 19 times in the Old Testament and twice in the New Testament. In Genesis 15:18 it is described as the eastern boundary of the land promised to Israel. An army, therefore, that crosses the Euphrates River from the east to the west invades the Promised Land.

The Euphrates River, most of which is in modern Iraq, has long been an important geographic barrier, and in the ancient world was second to none in importance. Its total length was some 1700 miles, and it was the main river of southwestern Asia, dividing the land geographically in much the same way the Mississippi River divides North America. So the river is significant historically, geographically, biblically, and prophetically.

To take Revelation 16:12 literally makes perfect sense. After all, one could reasonably expect that nations from the Far East would be involved in a world war culminating in the oil-rich Middle East. Thus, identifying the kings of the East with China, and possibly other nations such as India, fits the biblical evidence. The meteoric rise of China from a backward communist nation to an economic and military juggernaut fits in with the biblical alignment of the nations in the end times and serves as another key end-time signpost.

It's also fascinating that the Euphrates River appears to be drying up now, and the *New York Times* has noted the biblical significance of this. The front page of the July 13, 2009 edition had this stunning headline: "Iraq Suffers as the Euphrates River Dwindles." Not only did the *Times* mention the drying up of this historic river, it noted that Bible prophecy says this will happen in the last days of history, in the lead-up to the apocalyptic battle of Armageddon as described in the book of Revelation. Here's an excerpt from the article:

> Throughout the marshes, the reed gatherers, standing on land they once floated over, cry out to visitors in a passing boat. "Maaku mai!" they shout, holding up their rusty sickles. "There is no water!" The Euphrates is drying up. Strangled by the water policies of Iraq's neighbors, Turkey and Syria; a two-year drought; and years of misuse by Iraq and its farmers, the river is significantly smaller than it was just a few years ago. Some officials worry that it could soon be half of what it is now. The shrinking of the Euphrates, a river so crucial to the birth of civilization that the Book of Revelation prophesied its drying up as a sign of the end times, has decimated farms along its banks, has left fishermen impoverished and has depleted riverside towns as farmers flee to the cities looking for work.[2]

Is this an indication that events are falling into place for the coming of the kings of the East?

The King of the South

The final of the four end-time federations—the one that will occupy much of our focus in this book—is called "the king of the South" in Daniel 11:40. This appears to be the leader of Egypt, who directs a Muslim league of nations that will invade Israel at the same time as "the king of the North." We will discuss the king of the South in greater depth in chapters 5 and 6 and in the appendix.

The Nations Are in Place

According to Scripture, these are the four great confederations of nations that will exist during the end times. It appears that most of the nations of the world will be joined to one of these power blocs at one time or another. It's interesting that even today we can see the major nations of the world divided into these basic blocs. The western nations, centered in the US and Europe, are welded together by NATO. The rise of militant Islam has rallied the "king of the South." Russia, Iran, Turkey, and the nations of central Asia are strengthening their alliance in a federation located to the north of Israel. And the fact that China, and more recently North Korea, are major international players could easily be the precursor to the mighty "kings from the east" who pour into Israel for Armageddon (Revelation 16:12). J. Dwight Pentecost, writing back in 1971, succinctly summarized what was happening at the time. Think about how much farther we have gone down the road today.

> If in our day we can see the hand of God moving toward the completion of those programs that will

be fulfilled in the tribulation, and if the rapture has to take place before the fulfillment of these, who can say that the rapture could not take place right now? One would have to be spiritually blind or grossly ignorant to miss the fact that the hand of God is moving nations, raising up nations that historians said would never rise again, and bringing about alliances of nations and divisions among nations that historians and political scientists have said could never be accomplished. In the last twenty years more has happened in international affairs than has happened for two thousand years, and it has happened according to God's guidebook. God knew what He would do when He foretold what would take place in the end times.[3]

With each passing day, the picture on the top of the box seems to keep getting clearer and clearer!

Chapter 4

The Coming Middle East War

*Frustrated at their inability to profit from Israel's fortune
and determined to dominate and occupy the Holy Land,
the Russians had launched an attack against Israel in
the middle of the night. The assault became known as
the Russian Pearl Harbor... The number of aircraft and
warheads made it clear their mission was annihilation...*

*Miraculously, not one casualty was reported in all
of Israel. Otherwise Buck might have believed some
mysterious malfunction had caused missile and plane
to destroy each other. But witnesses reported that it
had been a firestorm, along with rain and hail and an
earthquake, that consumed the entire offensive effort.*

*Editors and readers had their own explanations for the
phenomenon, but Buck admitted, if only to himself, that
he became a believer in God that day. Jewish scholars
pointed out passages from the Bible that talked about God
destroying Israel's enemies with a firestorm, earthquake,
hail, and rain. Buck was stunned when he read Ezekiel
38 and 39 about a great enemy from the north invading
Israel with the help of Persia, Libya, and Ethiopia.*[1]

TIM LAHAYE AND JERRY JENKINS, *LEFT BEHIND*

There's a story I heard years ago about a group of Arab military troops who were gathered together near a hill. While there, they heard a voice from over the hill say, "One Jew can whip twenty-five Arabs." The Arabs were angered and sent twenty-five men over the hill. After a brief outburst of gunfire there was dead silence, and then the same voice, saying, "One Jew can whip fifty Arabs." Again the Arabs were incensed, and this time they sent fifty men over the hill. The sounds of fierce fighting rang out, then again there was silence. The same voice declared, "One Jew can whip one hundred Arabs." Filled with indignation, the Arabs sent one hundred of their crack troops over the hill, armed to the teeth. When all the commotion ceased on the other side of the hill, the Arabs saw one lone Arab soldier return over the hill in tattered clothes. He cried out, "Go back, go back—it's a trap. There are two of them!"

Of course that's a joke, but it serves to underscore the stunning success the Jewish people have experienced in the many wars the Arabs have instigated since the founding of the modern state of Israel. The Arab nations surrounding Israel have been in a declared state of war with Israel since May 14, 1948. Their stated goal is to drive the Jews into the sea, yet for all their sustained efforts, Israel today is stronger and more populated than ever before. Here is a brief overview of the ongoing hostilities between Israel and her Arab neighbors.

> 1948-49 When Israel officially became an independent state on May 14, 1948, she was immediately attacked from all sides by Egypt, Jordan, Iraq, Syria, Lebanon, and Saudi Arabia. When the truce was implemented in January 7, 1949, Israel had expanded her territory from 5000 square miles to 8000, including much of the Negev, the

huge desert to the south between Israel and Egypt.

1956 The Suez War between Egypt and Israel—Egyptian leader Gamal Abdel Nasser nationalized the Suez Canal. On October 29, 1956, Israel invaded the Sinai Peninsula and took control. Later, Israel returned the Sinai to Egypt.

1967 The famous Six-Day War (June 5-10)—Israel captured the Sinai Peninsula from Egypt, the West Bank from Jordan, the Golan Heights from Syria, and seized control of Jerusalem.

1973 The Yom Kippur War—On October 6, 1973, on Israel's most holy day, the Day of Atonement (Yom Kippur), Israel was attacked by Egypt and Syria. After heavy fighting, Israel repelled the invaders.

1982-85 The war with Lebanon.

2006 Israel waged a bloody 34-day war with Hezbollah and Hamas.

Even today, Israel remains on the cutting edge of new technology that could lead to greater security and protection. While recently there have been some chinks in the armor, Israel still has the most powerful military in the region and is always working to come up with better ways for defending itself. For example, the Israel Defense Forces have deployed a new cutting-edge antirocket system, called the Iron Dome. The system is designed to combat the rise in the number of rockets Palestinians have fired from Gaza.

> Iron Dome is a $200 million investment consisting of cameras, radar, launchers, and a control system. It tracks incoming rockets and is designed to strike down rockets within seconds of being launched. Previously, rockets have gone undetected by Israel's high-tech weaponry. Their short flight path, which takes only a few seconds, has made them difficult to track… The system is capable of detecting whether or not a rocket should be shot down. If a rocket is aimed for a remote area and is unlikely to result in casualties, the system will allow the rocket to land.[2]

This new defensive system is not foolproof and can't protect every location in Israel, but it does further reveal the kind of advanced military technology at Israel's disposal. Yet, in spite of Israel's ingenuity and proven ability to defend herself, according to the Bible, the greatest threat to Israel's continued existence has not yet occurred. While it may seem difficult to believe, Scripture says the Jewish people will one day face their greatest military test in what may be the very near future. One of the great events of the end times is an invasion of Israel by a vast horde of nations from every direction. This invasion, which is known as the Battle of Gog and Magog, is graphically described in Ezekiel 38–39. Taken literally, this passage predicts a last-days invasion of Israel from every direction by a massive, stampeding coalition of nations, and God's direct, supernatural intervention to annihilate the invaders. Events in the Middle East today strikingly foreshadow this coming invasion. The continued unrest and smoldering hatred for Israel are the perfect ingredients for what the Bible predicts.

To help us gain a clear understanding of Ezekiel 38–39 and how current events point toward the fulfillment of these chapters, we will use five standard questions of journalism: who, when, why, what, and how.

The Participants (Ezekiel 38:1-7): Who?

The prophecy about the battle of Gog and Magog begins with a list of ten proper names in 38:1-7, or what we might call God's "most-wanted list."

> The word of the LORD came to me saying, "Son of man, set your face toward Gog of the land of Magog, the prince of Rosh, Meshech and Tubal, and prophesy against him and say, 'Thus says the Lord GOD, "Behold, I am against you, O Gog, prince of Rosh, Meshech and Tubal. I will turn you about and put hooks into your jaws, and I will bring you out, and all your army, horses and horsemen, all of them splendidly attired, a great company with buckler and shield, all of them wielding swords; Persia, Ethiopia and Put with them, all of them with shield and helmet; Gomer with all its troops; Beth-togarmah from the remote parts of the north with all its troops—many peoples with you. Be prepared, and prepare yourself, you and

all your companies that are assembled about you, and be a guard for them"""" (Ezekiel 38:1-7).

The name *Gog*, which occurs 11 times in Ezekiel 38–39, is a name or title of the leader of the invasion. It is clear that Gog is an individual because several times, God addresses him directly (38:14; 39:1) and he is also called a prince (38:2; 39:1). It appears that the Group of Ten's bold move to make the peace treaty with Israel and her neighbors and consolidate absolute power over the Middle East will result in a disastrous countermove by Gog, the military leader of a coalition of Islamic nations and Russia.

The other nine proper names in Ezekiel 38:1-7 are specific geographical locations: Magog, Rosh, Meshech, Tubal, Persia, Cush (often translated as Ethiopia), Put, Gomer and Beth-togarmah. None of the place names mentioned in Ezekiel 38:1-7 exist on any modern map. Ezekiel used ancient place names that were familiar to the people of his day. While the names of these geographical locations have changed many times throughout history and may change again, the geographical territory remains the same. Regardless of what names they may carry at the time of this invasion, it is these specific geographical areas that will be involved. Each of these ancient geographical locations from Ezekiel's day will be briefly examined, and the modern counterpart will be identified.

Magog

According to the Jewish historian Josephus, the ancient Scythians inhabited the land of Magog.[3] The Scythians were northern nomadic tribes who inhabited territory from Central

Asia across the southern steppes of modern Russia. Magog today probably represents the former underbelly of the Soviet Union: Kazakhstan, Kirghizia, Uzbekistan, Turkmenistan, and Tajikistan. Afghanistan could also be part of this territory. All of these nations are dominated by Islam and have combined total population in excess of 60 million.

Rosh

Bible scholars have often identified Rosh with Russia. But this conclusion has not been unanimous. There are two key issues that must be resolved to properly interpret Rosh in Ezekiel 38–39: (1) Is Rosh a common noun or a name? And (2) Does Rosh have any relation to Russia?

Common Noun or Proper Name?

The first point that must be considered is whether the word "Rosh" in Ezekiel 38:2-3 and 39:1 NASB is a proper name or simply a common noun. The word *rosh* in Hebrew means "head, top, summit, or chief." It is a very common word and is used in all Semitic languages. It occurs over 600 times in the Old Testament. Many translations render *rosh* as a common noun and translate it as the word *chief*. The King James Version, Revised Standard Version, English Standard Version, New American Bible, New Living Translation, and the New International Version all adopt this translation. However, the Jerusalem Bible, New English Bible, and New American Standard Bible all translate *rosh* as a proper name, indicating a geographical location.

The weight of evidence favors taking *rosh* as a proper name in Ezekiel 38–39. There are five arguments that favor this view.

First, the eminent Hebrew scholars C.F. Keil and Wilhelm Gesenius both hold that the better translation of Rosh in Ezekiel 38:2-3 and 39:1 is as a proper noun referring to a specific geographical location.[4]

Second, the Septuagint, which is the Greek translation of the Old Testament, translates *rosh* as the proper name *Ros*. This is especially significant given the Septuagint was translated only three centuries after Ezekiel was written (obviously much closer to the writing of the original manuscript than any modern translation). The mistranslation of Rosh in many modern translations as an adjective can be traced to the Latin Vulgate of Jerome.[5]

Third, in their articles on *Rosh*, many Bible dictionaries and encyclopedias support taking it as a proper name in Ezekiel 38. Here are a few examples: *New Bible Dictionary, Wycliffe Bible Dictionary,* and *International Standard Bible Encyclopedia.*

Fourth, Rosh is mentioned the first time in Ezekiel 38:2 and then repeated in Ezekiel 38:3 and 39:1. If Rosh were simply a title, it would be dropped in the latter two places because when titles are repeated in Hebrew, they are generally abbreviated.

The fifth argument—and the most impressive evidence in favor of taking Rosh as a proper name—is simply that this translation is the most accurate. G.A. Cooke translates Ezekiel 38:2 "the chief of Rosh, Meshech and Tubal." He calls this "the most natural way of rendering the Hebrew."[6] The overwhelming evidence of biblical scholarship requires that Rosh be understood as a proper name, the name of a specific geographic area.

Is Rosh Russia?

Having established that Rosh should be taken as a proper name of a geographical area, the next task is to determine what geographical location is in view. There are three key reasons for understanding Rosh in Ezekiel 38–39 as a reference to Russia.

First, linguistically, there is evidence that Rosh is Russia. The great Hebrew scholar Wilhelm Gesenius noted, in the nineteenth century, that "Rosh is undoubtedly the Russians" (Gesenius died in 1842).[7]

Second, historically, there is substantial evidence that in Ezekiel's day there was a group of people known variously as Rash, Reshu, or Ros who lived in what today is southern Russia.[8]

Third, geographically, Ezekiel 38–39 emphasizes repeatedly that at least part of this invading force will come from the "remote parts of the north" (38:6,15) or "the remotest parts of the north" (39:2). Biblical directions are usually given in reference to the nation of Israel, which on God's compass is the center of the earth (Ezekiel 38:12). If you draw a line directly north from Israel, the land that is most remote or distant to the north is Russia. Therefore, it seems very likely that Russia will be the leader of the Gog coalition.

Meshech and Tubal

Meshech and Tubal are normally mentioned together in Scripture. In his notes in *The Scofield Study Bible* on Ezekiel 38:2, C.I. Scofield identified Meshech and Tubal as the Russian cities of Moscow and Tobolsk. Scofield wrote, "That the primary reference is to the northern (European) powers, headed up by Russia, all agree…The reference to Meshech and Tubal (Moscow and Tobolsk) is a clear mark of identification."

While the names do sound alike, this is not a proper method of identification. Meshech and Tubal are mentioned two other times in Ezekiel. In 27:13 they are mentioned as trading partners with ancient Tyre. In 32:26 their demise is recorded. It is highly unlikely that ancient Tyre (modern Lebanon) was trading with Moscow and the Siberian city of Tobolsk. The preferred identification is that Meshech and Tubal are the ancient Moschoi and Tibarenoi found in Greek writings or Tabal and Musku mentioned in Assyrian inscriptions. The ancient locations are in present-day Turkey. This is best understood as a reference to modern Turkey, an Islamic country.

Persia

The words "Persia," "Persian," or "Persians" are found 35 times in the Old Testament. In Ezekiel 38:5, "Persia" is best understood as modern-day Iran. The ancient land of Persia became the modern nation of Iran in March 1935, and then the name was changed to the Islamic Republic of Iran in 1979. Iran's present population is about 70 million. Iran's regime is the world's number one sponsor of terror. The nation is making its bid for regional supremacy at the same time it is pursuing nuclear weapons, and the president of Iran has declared that Israel must be wiped off the map. Clearly, modern Iran is hostile to Israel and the West. We'll deal more in-depth with Iran in the next chapter.

Ethiopia (Cush)

The Hebrew word *Cush* in Ezekiel 38:5 is often translated

"Ethiopia" in modern versions. Ancient Cush was called *Kusu* by the Assyrians and Babylonians, *Kos* or *Kas* by the Egyptians, and *Nubia* by the Greeks. Secular history locates Cush directly south of ancient Egypt, extending down past the modern city of Khartoum, which is the capital of modern Sudan. Thus, modern Sudan inhabits the ancient land of Cush.

Recently the nation split into two. Northern Sudan is a hard-line Islamic nation that supported Iraq during the Gulf War and harbored Osama bin Laden from 1991 to 1996. It is not surprising that this part of Africa would be hostile to the West and could easily join in an attack on Israel.

Southern Sudan, which is mostly Christian, became Africa's fifty-fourth nation in July 2011. A referendum for independence in January 2011 was approved by an almost unanimous vote. The fact Sudan has split into the Islamic north and mostly Christian south makes the fulfillment of Ezekiel's prophecy even more likely because the radical Islamic north can now act on its own. In light of the independence of southern Sudan, the Sudanese president Omar al Bashir stated that North Sudan will intensify its adherence to sharia law. He said, "If the south Sudan secedes, we will change the constitution and at that time there will be no time to speak of diversity of culture and ethnicity. sharia (Islamic law) and Islam will be the main source for the constitution, Islam the official religion and Arabic the official language."[9] North Sudan is poised to take its place in the coming Gog alliance just as Ezekiel predicted.

Libya (Put)

Some ancient sources indicate that *Put* or *Phut* was a North

African nation—with references documented in the Hebrew text footnotes in the *New Living Translation* for a number of passages, including Jeremiah 46:9; Ezekiel 27:10; 30:5; and Nahum 3:9. From the *Babylonian Chronicles*, which is a series of tablets recording ancient Babylonian history, it appears that *Putu* was the "distant" land to the west of Egypt, which would be modern-day Libya and could possibly include nations further west such as modern Algeria and Tunisia. The Septuagint, which was the first Greek translation of the Old Testament, renders the word *Put* as *Libues*.

Modern Libya, which is an Islamic nation, was under the rule of Colonel Muammar al-Gaddafi from 1969 to 2011. Libya remains a hardened Islamic state that hates Israel and despises the West, in spite of the 2011 US intervention with NATO in bombings and setting up a no-fly zone to protect rebel forces. We will discuss Libya in more detail in chapter 6.

Gomer

Gomer has often been identified by Bible teachers as Germany, or more particularly East Germany before the fall of communism. This identification is superficial and has no connection with the literal meaning of the word *Gomer* in its cultural and historic context. Gomer is probably a reference to the ancient Cimmerians or Kimmerioi. Ancient history identifies biblical Gomer with the Akkadian *Gi-mir-ra-a* and the Armenian *Gamir*. Beginning in the eighth century BC the Cimmerians occupied territory in Anatolia, which is located in modern Turkey. The historian Josephus noted that the Gomerites were identified with the Galatians, who inhabited what today is central Turkey.[10] Turkey is an Islamic nation with deepening ties with Russia. Turkey's natural allegiance is not with the EU but to her Muslim neighbors, and the nation has a formidable military presence on the northern border of Iraq.

Beth-togarmah

The Hebrew word *beth* means "house," so Beth-togarmah means the "house of Togarmah." Togarmah is mentioned in Ezekiel 27:14 as a nation that traded horses and mules with ancient Tyre. Ezekiel 38:6 states that the armies of Beth-togarmah will join in too, from the distant north. Ancient Togarmah was also known as Til-garamu (Assyrian) or Tegarma (Hittite), and its territory is in modern Turkey, which is north of Israel. Again, Turkey is identified as part of this group of nations that will attack Israel to challenge the Group of Ten.

THE GOG COALITION

Ancient Name	Modern Nation
Rosh (Rashu, Rasapu, Ros, and Rus)	Russia
Magog (Scythians)	Central Asia and possibly Afghanistan
Meshech (Moschoi and Musku)	Turkey
Tubal (Tabal)	Turkey
Persia	Iran
Ethiopia (Cush)	Sudan

Libya (Put or Phut)	Libya
Gomer (Cimmerians)	Turkey
Beth-togarmah (Til-garamu or Tegarma)	Turkey

Based on these identifications, Ezekiel 38–39 predicts an invasion of the land of Israel in the last days by a vast confederation of nations from north of the Black and Caspian Seas, extending down to modern Iran in the east, as far as modern Libya to the west, and down to Sudan in the south. Therefore, Russia will have at least five key allies: Turkey, Iran, Libya, Sudan, and the Islamic nations that came out of the former Soviet Union. Amazingly, all of these nations are Muslim, and Iran, Libya, and North Sudan are three of Israel's most ardent opponents.

Most of these same nations are hotbeds of militant Islam and are either forming or strengthening their ties with each other. This list of nations reads like the Who's Who of this week's news. It does not require a very active imagination to envision these nations openly challenging the West and conspiring together to invade Israel in the near future. And the prophet Ezekiel predicted all of this more than 2500 years ago. This is yet another powerful confirmation of the divine inspiration of the Bible. Who but God could ever make this kind of detailed prediction millennia before its fulfillment?

One thing you might have noticed as we went through this litany of names is the nations that are *not* listed. For instance, there's no specific mention of Egypt, Syria, Jordan, Lebanon, Saudi Arabia, or Iraq (ancient Babylon). These nations are very much in the headlines today. That raises a very legitimate question: Why are these nations not mentioned? There are several possible answers. First, these nations may be destroyed at some earlier time. That's the thesis of many prophecy teachers who posit an earlier "Psalm 83 war," in which the near enemies of Israel are destroyed before the Tribulation period begins. We will address this view in more detail in chapter 8.

A second explanation is that the nations nearest to Israel could be part of the future treaty the Antichrist will forge between Israel and her neighbors, similar to the agreements Israel currently has with Egypt and Jordan. The nations may be at some sort of so-called "peace" with Israel and decide not to participate in this invasion.

A third possibility is that these nations could be part of the invasion but not specifically mentioned as having part. At the very end of Ezekiel 38:6, after listing the allies in this assault, Ezekiel closes with the words "many peoples with you." Some believe this refers to other nations surrounding Israel that were not named earlier by Ezekiel. When one looks on a map, it's clear that the nations named in Ezekiel 38:1-6 are what we might call the "far enemies" of Israel. They represent the farthest enemies of Israel in every direction—Russia to the north, Iran to the east, Sudan to the south, and Libya to the west. It could be that Ezekiel lists the far nations and then includes the near enemies in the words "many peoples with you."

While any of these explanations are plausible, I believe that options two and three carry the most weight. We will consider the Psalm 83 war and the future of Syria in more detail in chapters 8 and 9.

The Period (Ezekiel 38:8): When?

One of the principal questions we can ask about the battle of Gog and Magog is this: When will it occur? The answer is given in Ezekiel 38:7-11,14,16:

> Be prepared, and prepare yourself, you and all your companies that are assembled about you, and be a guard for them. After many days you will be summoned; in the latter years you will come into the land that is restored from the sword, whose inhabitants have been gathered from many nations to the mountains of Israel which had been a continual waste; but its people were brought out from the nations, and they are living securely, all of them. "You will go up, you will come like a storm; you will be like a cloud covering the land, you and all your troops, and many peoples with you."
>
> Thus says the Lord GOD, "It will come about on that day, that thoughts will come into your mind and you will devise an evil plan, and you will say, 'I will go up against the land of unwalled villages I will go against those who are at rest, that live securely, all of them living without walls and having no bars or gates...'"
>
> Therefore prophesy, son of man, and say to Gog, "Thus says the Lord GOD, 'On that day when My people Israel are living securely, will you not know it?...and you will come up against My people Israel like a cloud to cover the land. It shall come about in the last days that I will bring you against My land, so

that the nations may know Me when I am sanctified through you before their eyes, O Gog.'"

Clearly, if one takes this passage with any degree of literalness, the events described did not occur in the past.[11] But could they happen soon? What indications do we have in Ezekiel 38–39 about the timing of this invasion? Several opinions have been offered by capable Bible scholars on this point, and there has been considerable disagreement. The invasion has been placed at almost every point in the end times by various scholars. Some feel the battle will take place before the rapture (this is the view held in the Left Behind™ series); others believe it will occur between the time of the rapture and the beginning of the Tribulation; still others say it will take place in connection with the battle of Armageddon at the end of the Great Tribulation. Some find it at the end of the millennium, pointing to a reference to Gog and Magog in Revelation 20:8. Others maintain that it will unfold in phases over the entire period of the Tribulation. Phase one (Ezekiel 38) will occur at the middle of the Tribulation, while phase two (Ezekiel 39) will transpire at the end of the Tribulation.

There isn't space or time here to cover all these views in greater detail and present their strengths and weaknesses. But it's important to remember that we're given some key hints within the text that suggest when this battle will take place. One of the first clues is the context of Ezekiel's prophecy. As John Phillips notes,

> The prophet put it between a discussion of the physical rebirth of the nation of Israel (chap. 37) and a long

> description of Israel's spiritual rebirth (chaps. 40-48).
> In other words, Russia's brief day of triumph lies some-
> where between those two crucial events...the prophet
> deliberately sandwiched Russia's "date with destiny"
> between Israel's political and spiritual rebirths.[12]

One of the clues given is that the battle will take place at a time when Israel has been regathered into its ancient land and is dwelling securely and at rest (Ezekiel 38:8,11,14).

There aren't too many times when Israel is at rest in God's prophetic program. The Jewish people have been scattered and persecuted over the face of the earth, and not even in the future will Israel have many periods of rest.

Some maintain that Israel is at rest and living securely today, and say this prophecy could be fulfilled at any time. I disagree. No matter how hard one might try to stretch the meaning of these words, Israel is not at rest today. Israel is an armed camp living under a tenuous truce with only two of her Arab neighbors—Egypt and Jordan—and both of those agreements could be in dire jeopardy in light of current events in the Middle East. The rest of Israel's neighbors would love nothing more than to drive every Israelite into the Mediterranean Sea. The reason they do not is because, humanly speaking, Israel has a good army that is more than a match for its neighbors.

Today an armed truce and a no-man's land separates Israel from her enemies. Every young Israeli man is required to have three years of military training, and every young Israeli woman is expected to have two years of military training. While the women are trained for jobs that are not necessarily combatant, they also learn to use weapons so that if they need to fight, they can. After military training, many of these men and women are settled in villages near the border, where they can serve a double purpose—follow their occupation, whatever it is, and serve as guards for the border of Israel.

This current state of unrest in Israel clearly does not correspond to Ezekiel's prophecy. If Russia and her varied allies should invade the Middle East today, it would not be a fulfillment of this portion of Scripture. That has to take place when Israel is at rest.

One point at which Israel will be at rest is during the millennial kingdom, or Christ's 1000-year reign here on earth. But we are expressly told that there will be no war during the millennial kingdom (Isaiah 2:4). Not until the rebellion occurs at the end of the millennium—when Satan is let loose (Revelation 20:7-9)—will war break out. Certainly Israel is not going to be at rest at the time Satan is let loose.

Some have suggested that Israel will be at rest during the Great Tribulation just before the second coming of Christ, and that Ezekiel's prophecy will be fulfilled at that time in conjunction with the battle of Armageddon. However, during the Great Tribulation, Israel will not be at rest, for Christ warned that when the Great Tribulation comes, the Israelites would need to flee to the mountains to escape their persecutors (Matthew 24:16). Therefore the invasion described by Ezekiel could not be a part of the battle of Armageddon.

There is only one period in the future that clearly fits Ezekiel's prophesied time of rest, and that is during the first half of Daniel's seventieth week of God's program for Israel (Daniel 9:27). After the church has been raptured and saints have been raised from the dead and Christians who are still alive on earth have been caught up to be with the Lord, a group of ten world leaders will lead a coalition of countries that comprise the same general territory held by the ancient Roman Empire. Out of the Group of Ten will come a strongman, the Antichrist, who will go on to become a world dictator. Daniel 9:26 refers to this ruler as "the prince who is to come." He will enter into a seven-year treaty of protection and peace with the people of Israel (verse 27).

Under that covenant, Israel will be able to relax, for her Gentile enemies will have become her friends, apparently guaranteeing her borders and promising her peace. Therefore, it seems the battle prophesied by Ezekiel will come when Israel has been lulled into the false security brought about by the peace agreement forged by the leader of the revived Roman Empire. This peace treaty will cause Israel to turn her energies toward increased wealth rather than defense—yet the peace treaty will be shattered less than four years later.

As John Phillips notes, "Only one period fits all the facts. When the Beast first comes to power in Europe, he will quickly unify the West, impose his totalitarian will on the nations under his control, and begin to prepare for world conquest. The major obstacle to his future plans will be a revitalized Russia." And I might add, an energized Islamic coalition. Phillips continues, "The invasion, then, takes place *after* the Rapture of the church, *after* the rise of the Beast in the West, *after* the signing of the pact with Israel, and just *before* the Beast takes over the world. Indeed it is the collapse of Russia [and the Islamic allies] that makes his global empire possible."[13] I agree.

The first three-and-a-half years of the seven-year Tribulation is the one time when regathered Israel will be at rest and secure. Apparently Russia and her Islamic allies will invade the land of Israel during that period, possibly toward its close, and Eze-kiel's prophecy will then be fulfilled.

The Purpose (Ezekiel 38:9-12): Why?

The fourth key issue addressed in Ezekiel 38–39 is the pur-pose of this invasion. Both the human and divine purposes for the invasion are given. The invading force will have four main goals: First, they will desire to acquire more territory. This is always part of any military invasion of this magnitude and scope, and this objective is implied in Ezekiel 38:8.

Second, they will come to plunder Israel and amass wealth (Ezekiel 38:12). One might wonder, *What wealth?* No one knows for sure, but recent discoveries of vast gas reserves off the coast of Israel could be part of the equation as fossil fuels become more scarce in the future and trigger energy wars. According to recent reports, Israel's present gas reserves are val-ued at $150 billion, with estimates expected to go much higher:

> The discovery of the Tamar and Leviathan fields in the eastern Mediterranean over the past years prom-ises to transform an economy that is already grow-ing rapidly thanks to a booming high-tech sector and strong private sector investment. But while Israel may be relishing the prospect of running sovereign wealth investment like Middle East contemporaries Abu Dhabi, Qatar or Kuwait, officials are quick to emphasize that they are not about to abandon their

high-tech, export-driven growth model. "What is the value already discovered in the gas fields? In today's prices, Israel has $150 billion," Steinitz told Reuters in an interview in Brussels, where he was on his way to Paris for a meeting of the OECD, the club of wealthy nations that Israel recently joined. That figure—equivalent to 75 percent of Israel's gross domestic product—may be vast, but it could easily be exceeded, with drilling having so far only taken place in 20-25 percent of the country's economic waters, Steinitz said.[14]

Make no mistake: Greed and jealousy will be a key part of the motivation behind the Gog invasion.

Third, the invading horde will come to destroy the people of Israel and wipe them off the face of the earth (Ezekiel 38:10,16). This is in keeping with the hatred of the Jewish people that is manifest today by Israel's neighbors.

Fourth, these nations will attack to confront and challenge the Antichrist, or the king of the West, who will be Israel's ally as a result of the treaty mentioned in Daniel 9:27. Their attack on Israel will also be an attack against the Western confederacy.

While the nations that attack Israel will have their evil intent, God will also have His purpose as well. He says that through this attack He will be sanctified in the eyes of the nations:

> Therefore prophesy, son of man, and say to Gog, "Thus says the Lord GOD, 'On that day when My people Israel are living securely, will you not know it? You will come from your place out of the remote parts of the north, you and many peoples with you, all of them

riding on horses, a great assembly and a mighty army; and you will come up against My people Israel like a cloud to cover the land. It shall come about in the last days that I will bring you against My land, so that the nations may know Me when I am sanctified through you before their eyes, O Gog'" (Ezekiel 38:14-16).

The Product (Ezekiel 38:13-23): What?

When the invading force comes into Israel, there will be no stopping them. They will be bent on war and destruction. It will look like the perfect time to destroy Israel, and they will not back down. When these nations invade, it will look like the biggest mismatch in history. It will make the Arab invasions of Israel in 1967 and 1973 pale in comparison. When the leader of this army assembles this last-days strike force, it will look like Israel is finished. The Jewish people will be completely surrounded and will not be able to overcome their enemies by their own strength and ingenuity. Gog and his army will cover Israel like a cloud.

According to the Bible, it's at this time that God will come to the rescue of His people. Almighty God will intervene to win the battle. Ezekiel 38–39 describes what we might call the One-Day War or even the One-Hour War or "When Gog meets God" because God will quickly and completely annihilate the Islamic invaders from the face of the earth by supernatural means. Here is Ezekiel's graphic description of what will happen:

> "It will come about on that day, when Gog comes against the land of Israel," declares the Lord GOD,

"that My fury will mount up in My anger. In My zeal and in My blazing wrath I declare that on that day there will surely be a great earthquake in the land of Israel. The fish of the sea, the birds of the heavens, the beasts of the field, all the creeping things that creep on the earth, and all the men who are on the face of the earth will shake at My presence; the mountains also will be thrown down, the steep pathways will collapse, and every wall will fall to the ground. I will call for a sword against him on all My mountains," declares the Lord God. "Every man's sword will be against his brother. With pestilence and with blood I will enter into judgment with him; and I will rain on him, and on his troops, and on the many peoples who are with him, a torrential rain, with hailstones, fire, and brimstone. I will magnify Myself, sanctify Myself, and make Myself known in the sight of many nations; and they will know that I am the Lord" (38:18-23).

God will mount up in His fury to destroy these godless invaders. He will come to rescue His helpless people using four means to totally destroy Russia and her Islamic allies:

1. A great earthquake (38:19-20)—According to Jesus, the coming Tribulation will be a time of many terrible earthquakes (Matthew 24:7). And this specific earthquake will be used by God to conquer and confuse Israel's invaders.

2. Infighting among the troops of the various nations (38:21)—In the chaos after the powerful

earthquake, the armies of the invading nations represented will turn against each other. Think about it: The troops from the various invading countries will speak Russian, Farsi (Persian), Arabic, and Turkic languages. They will probably begin to kill anyone they can't identify. This could be the largest case of death by friendly fire in human history.

3. Disease (38:22a)—Gog and his troops will experience a horrible, lethal plague that will add to the misery and devastation already inflicted.

4. Torrential rain, hailstones, fire, and burning sulfur (38:22b)—Just as God poured fire from heaven upon Sodom and Gomorrah, He will send rain, hail, fire, and burning sulfur upon the invading army.

The invading nations will arrogantly swoop down on Israel to take her land, but the only land they will claim in Israel will be their burial plots (Ezekiel 39:12). They will set out to bury Israel, but God will end up burying them.

The Prophetic Significance: How?

The final question to consider is how the world stage today is being set for the fulfillment of this incredible prophecy. What are some of the key developments we are witnessing today that point toward this invasion? What recent or current events correspond with Ezekiel's prophecy? There are several that we will consider in chapters 5-7, but for now let's look at one particular event.

One of the more fascinating events that occurred took place in 1967 when Israel came to occupy the mountains in her land. According to Ezekiel 39:2-4, Israel must have possession of the "mountains of Israel" when this invasion occurs. There, God tells the future invaders:

> I will turn you around and lead you on, bringing you from the far north, and bring you against the mountains of Israel. Then I will knock the bow out of your left hand, and cause the arrows to fall out of your right hand. You shall fall upon the mountains of Israel, you and all your troops and the peoples who are with you; I will give you to birds of prey of every sort and to the beasts of the field to be devoured (NKJV).

The famous Six-Day War in Israel in 1967 helped set the stage for Ezekiel 39:2-4 to be fulfilled. Before the Six-Day War, all the mountains of Israel, with the exception of a small strip of West Jerusalem, were entirely in the hands of the Jordanian Arabs. Only since 1967 have the mountains *of* Israel been *in* Israel, thus making the fulfillment of Ezekiel's prophecy possible.

In the next chapter we'll look at some of other tectonic changes that have occurred in Egypt and Libya—changes that could foreshadow what's coming, maybe very soon.

Chapter 5

Egypt and the Rise of the King of the South

You can't make war in the Middle East without Egypt.[1]
HENRY KISSINGER

E gypt dominated the news for months in early 2011 and continues to be scrutinized by a watching world. All eyes are on this nation. The images are fresh in our minds—disturbing scenes of unrest, upheaval, and uprising. The discord first erupted in Tunisia, then spread to Egypt. Jordan and Yemen were next, followed by Libya and Syria, and even Saudi Arabia seems vulnerable. The world is facing a rising wave of uncertainty in the Middle East, and as a result, people are raising all kinds of questions—especially in relation to Egypt:

- *What does this mean for oil prices?* Eight percent of the world's seaborne commerce flows through the Suez Canal every day.

- *Who will ultimately replace Mubarak?* Egypt is the largest, most powerful Arab state in the Middle East.

- *Will the Muslim Brotherhood or other radical Islamist groups seize power in Egypt? Or at least have some role in the new government?*
- *When all the dust finally settles, how will the ongoings in Egypt affect its relationship with Israel?*

Though no one knows the answers to all these questions or what twists and turns events may take in the Middle East, the Bible does provide a sketch of what awaits Egypt's future.

Egypt and the Bible

Few people are probably aware that the words "Egypt," "Egyptian," and "Egyptians" appear about 850 times in the Bible. Of these 850 mentions, 250 verses in the Old Testament contain prophecies that, at the time they were given, were about events yet to take place in Egypt. This fact alone gives Egypt an important place in Bible prophecy. And the five main prophetic Bible passages dealing with Egypt are Isaiah 11:15-16; Isaiah 19:1-25; Jeremiah 46; Ezekiel 29–32; and Daniel 11:40-43. I would encourage you to read each of these passages. They describe three main future periods in Egypt's history: the present age, the Tribulation age, and the millennial age, or the 1000-year kingdom of Christ on earth.

Bible teachers have pointed out Egypt's significant place in Bible prophecy for many years. In 1957, Wilbur Smith wrote a 256-page book titled *Egypt in Biblical Prophecy*. Dr. John Walvoord wrote *The Nations in Prophecy* in 1967 and said, "The Scriptures reveal that Egypt will have a place in the future. Egypt will be one of the nations which figure in the final world conflict and will be the leader of the African forces."[2] Writing in 1970 in *The Late Great Planet Earth*, Hal Lindsey said, "The Bible says that Egypt, the Arabic nations, and countries of Africa will form an alliance, a sphere of power which will be called the King of the South. Allied with Russia, the King of the North, this formidable confederacy will rise up against the restored state of Israel."[3] Dr. J. Dwight Pentecost, in his 1971 book *Will Man Survive?* wrote, "How long ago in history did Egypt rise out of the dust of nations to take a significant place in world affairs? Not more than a decade ago…Out of the insignificant place among the nations, she has come to dominate the Middle East. Thus this group of nations has come together under the authority of Egypt, the one called the king of the south in Daniel 11."[4]

So, for some time now prophecy teachers have said Egypt will play a key role in end-time events. But what's transpiring today is unprecedented. Thus, I believe we need to take a fresh look at Egypt in prophecy in light of current events. To help us get a handle on what's happening now and where it's all headed, I want to gather our thoughts on Egypt around three simple points: (1) Egypt past, (2) Egypt present, and (3) Egypt future. As we survey these points, our main focus will be on Egypt future.

Egypt Past

Egypt has a long and glorious history. It's the land of the Pharaohs and the pyramids. The Greek historian Herodotus called Egypt the gift of the Nile. In the Bible, the first specific mention of Egypt is in Genesis 12.

Egypt instituted the world's first national government. The

nation's religion was obsessed with life after death. The people created expressive and expansive art and literature. They introduced complex stone architecture to the world. They produced the first convenient writing material, papyrus, made from the bulrush plant. They developed a 365-day calendar. And they pioneered breakthroughs in the fields of geometry and medical surgery.[5]

Egypt was a great world power until the sixth century BC, at which time it began to slide into decline. This descent was predicted in Scripture in Ezekiel 29:15, written in about 570 BC. There, Ezekiel said that Egypt would never again rule over the nations—that it would be "the lowest of the kingdoms." This has been proven true over time. After Persia's rise to power, Egypt never again was a major, independent international power. Egypt was successively ruled over by Greece, Rome, the Saracens, the Mamelukes, the Turks, and the British. Until 1922, Egypt remained under the sovereignty of a foreign power. The fact Egypt is its own sovereign nation today is an indication that we are approaching the last days, when she will once again have a significant role in world history.

Egypt became an independent nation in 1922 when it gained independence from Great Britain. At that time, a monarchy was instituted. When the modern state of Israel was formed in 1948, Egypt was joined by five other countries in the fight against the Jewish nation: Jordan, Iraq, Syria, Lebanon, and Saudi Arabia. The Egyptian monarchy lasted 30 years (until 1952). Then the military seized control of the country in a coup, and General Gamal Abdel Nasser became president. Nasser led the resurgence of Pan-Arab aspirations, fostering hopes of a glorious Arab golden age. He fought the Suez War with Israel in 1956, and the Six-Day War in June 1967 along with his allies, Jordan and Syria. When Nasser died in 1970, Anwar Sadat assumed power. Under Sadat, Egypt and Syria fought the Yom Kippur War against Israel in October 1973. In 1979, President Jimmy Carter brokered the Camp David Accords between President Sadat and Israeli prime minister Menachem. The agreement brought at least a cessation of war between the two nations. When Sadat was assassinated in 1981, he was succeeded by Hosni Mubarak, the man who was in the crosshairs of the recent chaos in Egypt.

Egypt Present

Egypt has dominated the news in recent months—the 18-day uprising, the clamoring crowds gathering day after day in Tahrir Square. The mounting pressure was so great that President Mubarak grudgingly relinquished power on February 11, 2011. His departure from office sparked nationwide celebrations. Since then, people everywhere have been asking: Are today's events in Egypt a fulfillment of ancient biblical prophecy? For help with an answer, we need to turn to Isaiah 19, where we find the Bible's most detailed prophecies about Egypt's future. I encourage you to read this chapter before we begin to unfold its meaning:

> The oracle concerning Egypt. Behold, the LORD is riding on a swift cloud and is about to come to Egypt; the idols of Egypt will tremble at His presence, and the heart of the Egyptians will melt within them. "So I will incite Egyptians against Egyptians; and they

will each fight against his brother and each against his neighbor, city against city and kingdom against kingdom. Then the spirit of the Egyptians will be demoralized within them; and I will confound their strategy, so that they will resort to idols and ghosts of the dead and to mediums and spiritists. Moreover, I will deliver the Egyptians into the hand of a cruel master, and a mighty king will rule over them," declares the Lord God of hosts.

The waters from the sea will dry up, and the river will be parched and dry. The canals will emit a stench, the streams of Egypt will thin out and dry up; the reeds and rushes will rot away. The bulrushes by the Nile, by the edge of the Nile and all the sown fields by the Nile will become dry, be driven away, and be no more. And the fishermen will lament, and all those who cast a line into the Nile will mourn, and those who spread nets on the waters will pine away. Moreover, the manufacturers of linen made from combed flax and the weavers of white cloth will be utterly dejected. And the pillars of Egypt will be crushed; all the hired laborers will be grieved in soul.

The princes of Zoan are mere fools; the advice of Pharaoh's wisest advisers has become stupid. How can you men say to Pharaoh, "I am a son of the wise, a son of ancient kings"? Well then, where are your wise men? Please let them tell you, and let them understand what the Lord of hosts has purposed against Egypt. The princes of Zoan have acted foolishly, the princes of Memphis are deluded; those who are the cornerstone of her tribes have led Egypt astray. The Lord has mixed within her a spirit of distortion; they have led Egypt astray in all that it does, as a drunken man staggers in his vomit. There will be no work for Egypt which its head or tail, its palm branch or bulrush, may do.

In that day the Egyptians will become like women, and they will tremble and be in dread because of the waving of the hand of the Lord of hosts, which He is going to wave over them. The land of Judah will become a terror to Egypt; everyone to whom it is mentioned will be in dread of it, because of the purpose of the Lord of hosts which He is purposing against them.

In that day five cities in the land of Egypt will be speaking the language of Canaan and swearing allegiance to the Lord of hosts; one will be called the City of Destruction. In that day there will be an altar to the Lord in the midst of the land of Egypt, and a pillar to the Lord near its border. It will become a sign and a witness to the Lord of hosts in the land of Egypt; for they will cry to the Lord because of oppressors, and He will send them a Savior and a Champion, and He will deliver them. Thus the Lord will make Himself known to Egypt, and the Egyptians will know the Lord in that day. They will even worship with sacrifice and offering, and will make a vow to the Lord and perform it. The Lord will strike Egypt, striking but healing; so they will return to the LORD, and He will respond to them and will heal them.

In that day there will be a highway from Egypt to Assyria, and the Assyrians will come into Egypt and the Egyptians into Assyria, and the Egyptians will worship with the Assyrians.

In that day Israel will be the third party with Egypt and Assyria, a blessing in the midst of the earth, whom the LORD of hosts has blessed, saying, "Blessed is Egypt My people, and Assyria the work of My hands, and Israel My inheritance."

So what part of this prophecy concerning Egypt has already been fulfilled, and what remains unfulfilled or is being fulfilled before our eyes? In the wake of the uprisings that took place in early 2011, some teachers maintained that Isaiah 19:1-4 was coming to pass right in front of us—that what we were seeing on the news every day looked eerily similar to Isaiah's prophecy:

The oracle concerning Egypt. Behold, the LORD is riding on a swift cloud and is about to come to Egypt; the idols of Egypt will tremble at His presence, and the heart of the Egyptians will melt within them. "So I will incite Egyptians against Egyptians; and they will each fight against his brother and each against his neighbor, city against city and kingdom against kingdom. Then the spirit of the Egyptians will be demoralized within them; and I will confound their strategy, so that they will resort to idols and ghosts of the dead and to mediums and spiritists. Moreover, I will deliver the Egyptians into the hand of a cruel master, and a mighty king will rule over them," declares the Lord GOD of hosts.

I received many email inquiries asking me about this passage during the Egyptian uprising, and many other emails from people claiming that this prophecy was being fulfilled at the time. This highlights a kind of error we must be careful to avoid when it comes to Bible prophecy. It's often called "newspaper exegesis"—that is, seeing something in the news headlines and then finding a biblical passage to support it. Clearly, the last part of Isaiah 19:2 was not fulfilled during the unrest of spring 2011. City was not fighting against city, nor was kingdom fighting against kingdom. We must be consistent in our interpretation and application of Scripture—we can't take part of a verse and view it as being fulfilled if the context doesn't allow for such.

I believe Isaiah 19:1-4 was fulfilled in 670 BC, when the Assyrians conquered Egypt. This passage was fulfilled almost 2700 years ago. What we have been seeing and are seeing today in Egypt is *not* the direct fulfillment of any biblical prophecy; however, these events certainly are bringing dramatic changes to the landscape of the Middle East and setting the stage for future happenings. Thus, what we see today is not a *fulfillment* of Bible prophecy, but a *foreshadowing* of what's to come.

Hal Lindsey, in *The Late Great Planet Earth*, said it well back in 1970:

> Current events in the Middle East have prepared the stage for Egypt's last act in the great drama which will

climax with the finale, Christ's personal return to earth. We are not attempting to read into today's happenings any events to prove some vague thesis. This is not necessary. All we need to do is know the Scriptures in their proper context and then watch with awe while men and countries, movements and nations, fulfill the roles that God's prophets said they would.[6]

He's right. We can sit back with awe and watch it all come together. We can see how events taking place today strikingly foreshadow what the biblical prophets said would come to pass.

With that in mind, there are three significant ways we see the groundwork for the end times being laid today by events in the Middle East in general and in Egypt in particular.

Peace Is the Key

First, current events in Egypt point toward the peace treaty of Daniel 9:27, which the Antichrist will forge between Israel and her neighbors. This treaty will mark the beginning of the seven-year Tribulation (Daniel 9:27). The world is desperately yearning for peace in the Middle East, and the current turmoil is magnifying that desperation and desire. Calls for some kind of regional peace agreement will continue to swell as the unrest and uncertainty in Egypt and the rest of the Middle East continues to escalate.

Growing Globalism

Second, the Egyptian revolution is a vivid illustration of the globalism that points toward the end times. Think about it: 100 years ago, or even 50 years ago, people in the United States couldn't have cared less what happened in Egypt. Of course, we don't like to see people suffer in any part of the world, but politically, what took place in Egypt back then didn't have much impact on our lives. Back in those days, we probably would have never even heard about what was taking place.

But today's globalism has changed all that. Now, when something happens in one corner of the world, it has immediate and dramatic repercussions everywhere else. We all can watch it unfold 24/7 on cable news. The fact that we are even discussing the crisis in Egypt and other Middle East and North African nations proves that globalism is the new reality. It is this globalism—predicted in Scripture—that will make it possible for one man to rule the world someday. We are now going "back to Babel" (Genesis 11)—the whole world was together back then, and the same is happening again today.

Egypt vs. Israel…Again

Third, the current uprising in Egypt and its uncertain aftermath could push the nation closer to a showdown with Israel—a showdown the Bible predicts will happen in the future. While the West is issuing endless calls for peace, it looks possible that, in the near future, Egypt will break the treaty Mubarak signed with Israel in 1979. This would plunge Egypt and Israel back into an openly adversarial posture. According to recent reports, "More than half of all Egyptians would like to see the 1979 peace treaty with Israel annulled. According to results of a poll conducted by the U.S.-based Pew Research Center… According to the poll results, only 36 percent of Egyptians are in favor of maintaining the treaty, compared with 54 percent who would like to see it scrapped."[7]

Newsweek reports that 70 percent of Egyptians want to amend or cancel the Camp David Accords, and 27 percent believe that a Muslim Brotherhood majority would be a good thing.[8]

The New York Times also sounds the alarm about future relations between Israel and Egypt:

> Egypt is charting a new course in its foreign policy that has already begun shaking up the established order in the Middle East, planning to open the blockaded border with Gaza and normalizing relations with two of Israel and the West's Islamist foes, Hamas and Iran. Egyptian officials, emboldened by the revolution and with an eye on coming elections, say that they are moving toward policies that more accurately reflect public opinion. In the process they are seeking to reclaim the influence over the region that waned as their country became a predictable ally of Washington and the Israelis in the years since the 1979 peace treaty with Israel.[9]

The implications of all the Middle East upheaval are monumental for Israel, but nowhere is it more critical than in Egypt. In May 2011, in an act against Israel, Egypt re-opened the border into Gaza that had been closed by Israel and Egypt in 2007 when Hamas took control of Gaza. This has heightened concern in Israel that terrorists and vast amounts of weapons will now flow freely into Gaza.

Israel, then, appears to be confronting an ominous new threat. Almost every action Egypt is taking is signaling a return to the pre-Camp David Accords posture. Israel is also presently at peace with Jordan, but that agreement may also be on thin ice if uprisings in Jordan take hold in a serious way or if Jordan is pressured by other Arab nations to break the treaty. In recent decades, Israel has only had to worry about the threat from the north and to a lesser degree from the west in Gaza. If the treaty with Egypt unravels as a result of changes to the government, the southern flank of Israel would once again become a major menace. Many people are not aware that Egypt has the tenth largest military in the world (based on the number of active troops, which is 468,000). The United States pours $3.5 million a day into the Egyptian military, buying it everything from F-16 jets to M-1 tanks.[10] The possibility of a new threat from Egypt, then, is grave news indeed for Israel.

In the aftermath of the uprising in Egypt, Dennis Prager offered his thoughts in an article titled "Eight Reasons Not to Be Optimistic About Egypt." Here's what he said:

> From the moment the Tahrir Square demonstrations against Hosni Mubarak began, optimism has dominated American reporting and commentary on what is being called the Egyptian revolution. I fervently hope I am wrong, but I find it hard to share this dominant view, even as I identify with all those Egyptians and other Arabs who yearn for freedom.
>
> I offer eight good reasons for my pessimism:
>
> 1. Countries almost never go straight from dictatorship to liberty.
>   For the past 250 years, the general rule of revolutions

has been this: The more tyrannical the regime that is overthrown, the more tyrannical the regime that replaces it.

2. When pro-American dictators are overthrown, far more repressive anti-American tyrants usually replace them.

3. Islamists have a near-monopoly on passion in Egypt and elsewhere in the Arab world.

   In politics, passion matters. That is why small impassioned groups can dominate a more passive majority of a country. And in Egypt, no group or cause has nearly the passion that the Islamists have.

4. Neither liberty nor tolerance has roots in the Arab world.

   It is very hard, perhaps impossible, to plant the trees of liberty and tolerance in soil that has never grown them. And if these trees are planted, they are likely to take many years to grow.

5. People have been trained to depend on the state.

6. The American media have been hiding the bad guys.

   You have not been getting the whole truth about Tahrir Square. To this day, the print edition of *The New York Times* has not reported the sexual assault on Lara Logan, the chief CBS TV foreign correspondent, by 200 Egyptian men in Tahrir Square yelling "Jew, Jew" while they assaulted her. CBS News itself did not report on the incident until others exposed it. Likewise, few mainstream news media have reported or shown the depictions of Mubarak as an Israeli agent or attacks on other Western news teams accused of being agents of Israel.

7. Getting closer to Iran.

In one of its first actions after taking over control of the Egyptian government, the Egyptian army allowed two Iranian warships to sail through the Suez Canal for the first time since the Iranian revolution. If that is not a bad sign, nothing is.

8. Egypt is saturated with Jew and Israel hatred.

Finally, and arguably most significantly, Egypt and the rest of the Arab world have been swimming in a sea of Jew and Israel hatred for decades. Historically, anti-Semitism has been a perfect predictor of a society that will cause others problems and that will eventually self-destruct. The preoccupation with destroying Israel has been the single greatest obstacle to Arab countries joining the modern world. No Arab progress will be possible until the Arab world gives up its obsession with Israel's disappearance.[11]

Many are optimistic that Egypt's elections will bring a secular, democratic government to power in Egypt. But *what will democracy in Egypt look like?* It's not very promising. In a recent Pew Research poll done among Egyptians, it was discovered that...

- 77 percent favor whipping and cutting off hands as the punishment for robbery
- 84 percent favor the death penalty for Muslims who change their religion

- 82 percent think stoning adulterers is a good idea
- 50 percent view Hamas favorably

This isn't very encouraging for Egypt's future or its relations with Israel. Many fear that radical groups like the Muslim Brotherhood will surge to power, making the government even more repressive and anti-American. The slogan of the Muslim Brotherhood is very terse and yet telling: "Islam is the solution." The group condemned the "assassination" of Osama bin Laden by Navy Seals in Pakistan, warned the US to stop interfering in the internal affairs of any Arab or Muslim nation, and called on the West, especially the US, to stop linking Islam with terrorism.

One sign of the Brotherhood's increasing acceptance and official legitimacy within Egypt occurred when the military government appointed a panel of experts to draw up changes to the Egyptian Constitution and included one member from the group, which had formerly been banned from having a voice in government affairs. According to *The New York Times*,

> In the 2005 elections, the Brotherhood won 88 seats in Parliament, or about 20 percent of the total, but the Mubarak government pushed the group out of the country's most recent vote last fall, in elections that were widely seen as fraudulent. The constitutional amendments to be drawn up in the coming days are widely expected to include broadening the terms of eligibility for political participation, including allowing the Brotherhood to compete under its own name as a party.[12]

Egypt is headed down a path that is consistent with what the Bible predicts about its future. While all the lingering political questions are interesting and important, it's time for us to turn our attention now to the prophetic questions. And for the answers, we'll look at what God's Word says.

Egypt Future

According to Scripture, there are two key time periods in Egypt's future—the Tribulation years, and the millennium. Let's look first at what the Bible says will happen to Egypt during the coming seven-year Tribulation.

Egypt in the Tribulation

The first key prophecies about Egypt's future are found in Daniel 11:40, which says, "At the end time the king of the South will collide with him, and the king of the North will storm against him with chariots, with horsemen and with many ships; and he will enter countries, overflow them and pass through." It's important at this point to look at the context and background of Daniel 11.

This chapter is one of the most remarkable in the Old Testament. It contains an astonishing prophecy that Bible teachers and commentators have stated is of great significance. For example, John Walvoord said, "Probably no other portion of Scripture presents more minute prophecy than Daniel 11:1-35, and this has prompted the sharpest attack of critics seeking to discredit this prophetic portion."[13] Joyce Baldwin observed, "If he accepts as axiomatic the fact of foretelling in the Bible as a whole and therefore in this book, nowhere else is prediction as specific and detailed as here."[14] Warren Wiersbe called it a "Remarkable Prophecy."[15] H.A. Ironside stated that the minute details in Daniel 11 validate "the absolute unerring precision of God's holy word" and demonstrate that "all history is His story."[16] Leon Wood stated, "The details of this history as presented provide one of the most remarkable predictive portions of all of Scripture."[17]

Daniel 11:1-35 contains an extraordinarily detailed preview of world history. According to scholars, there are at least 100 prophecies and possibly as many as 135 in Daniel 11:1-35 that have been fulfilled and can be corroborated by a careful study of history.[18] Daniel 11:5-20 alone chronicles the 150-year struggle (320-170 BC) between the Ptolemaic (Egyptian) and Seleucid (Syrian) dynasties, which were broken off from Alexander the Great's mighty empire. Of course, the nation caught in the middle of this power struggle was Israel, which is God's focal point in all this. In Daniel 11:21 we read of one key individual, Antiochus IV, also known as Epiphanes, which means "god manifest." The Jews, however, called him Epimanes, which means "madman."

Antiochus was a Syrian king who serves as a type, a prototype, a foreshadow, a haunting harbinger of the ultimate world ruler of the end times. He was an evil ruler who systematically slaughtered and enslaved as many as 80,000 Jews. He desecrated the Jewish temple and erected a monument within it known as "the abomination of desolation" (Daniel 11:31), probably a statue of Zeus that just happened to look like Antiochus. The precious Torah scrolls were destroyed, Sabbath observance and circumcision were forbidden, and unclean swine's flesh was forced down the throats of the Jewish priests. This precipitated the legendary Maccabean revolt (Daniel 11:32-34) that brought about the restoration of the temple and led to the establishment of the Jewish Feast of Lights, or Hanukkah.

Then in Daniel 11:36, Antiochus suddenly fades into the background and the Antichrist comes into full view. At Daniel 11:36, history ends and prophecy begins. We skip over a long era of time to last-days events and find a chilling portrait of the king of the West—the Antichrist—and the confederacy he leads. The events recorded in this section of Daniel will occur during the coming seven-year Tribulation, or after all believers in Christ have been caught up to heaven through the rapture.

This means the world has already had a preview or sneak peek of the Antichrist in the person of Antiochus Epiphanes. Daniel 11:36 leaps from the time of Antiochus and the Maccabean period to the time of the Antichrist, and verses 37-39 go on to tell us more about the Antichrist:

> The king will do as he pleases, and he will exalt and magnify himself above every god and will speak monstrous things against the God of gods; and he will prosper until the indignation is finished, for that which is decreed will be done. He will show no regard for the gods of his fathers or for the desire of women, nor will he show regard for any other god; for he will magnify himself above them all. But instead he will honor a god of fortresses, a god whom his fathers did not know; he will honor him with gold, silver, costly stones and treasures. He will take action against the strongest of fortresses with the help of a foreign god;

he will give great honor to those who acknowledge
him and will cause them to rule over the many, and
will parcel out land for a price (Daniel 11:36-39).

We know this refers to the future Antichrist because Antiochus never fulfilled the prophecies of Daniel 11:36-45. Also,
the text specifically indicates that these verses concern the end
times. Daniel 11:35 ends with the words "until the end time;
because it is still to come at the appointed time," and Daniel
11:36 opens with the word "Then"—that is, in the end time.
Between Daniel 11:35 and 36 we leap over the intervening
centuries from Antiochus, the man who foreshadows the final
Antichrist, to the final world ruler himself. This futurist interpretation is further confirmed in Daniel 11:40, which begins
with the words, "And at the end time."

Let me add here that Daniel 11:1-35 is critical to our understanding and interpretation of biblical prophecy. Looking back
in history, we can confirm that these prophecies were completely and literally fulfilled. It just makes sense that if the
prophecies of Daniel 11:1-35 were literally fulfilled down to
the last detail, then we can rest assured that the future prophecies of Daniel 11:36–12:3 will also be completely and literally
fulfilled as well, possibly very soon.

In Daniel 11:40, the words "At the end time" are a clear
eschatological reference. As we have already seen, the Bible
presents four great power blocs of nations in the end times,
with each described in reference to their direction from Israel:
king of the West, king of the South, king of the North, kings of
the East. At least three of these powers are mentioned in Daniel
11:40-45. Daniel 11:40 begins by mentioning the "king of the

South," who will come against the Antichrist in the end times. I believe the king of the South refers to Egypt and some of its North African allies. How can we know this? The context tells us. The king of the South is mentioned seven times in Daniel 11:5-35, and in each case it refers to the ruler of Egypt under the ancient Ptolemies. With this clear historical pattern, and the fact that Egypt is to the south and west of Israel, it makes sense that the end-time king of the South in Daniel 11:40 will also be Egypt.

I believe that Daniel 11:40-43 parallels Ezekiel 38–39. While there are some differences between the two passages, both involve an attack by a massive north-south coalition of nations (with Libya [Put] and Sudan [Cush] specifically mentioned in both texts), both invasions occur during the first half of the coming Tribulation, and both directly involve Israel.

	EZEKIEL 38–39	**DANIEL 11:40-43**
Participants	Northern and southern alliance of nations (Libya and Sudan [Cush] specifically mentioned)	King of the South and king of the North (Libya and Sudan [Cush] specifically mentioned)
Period	First half of the Tribulation	First half of the Tribulation
Place	Armies destroyed in Israel	Antichrist invades Israel

It is difficult for me to imagine two completely different battles transpiring in such a short time in the same general area.[19] That's why I believe both passages refer to the same event.

The main difference is that Daniel 11:40-41 presents the attack by a great north-south coalition against the Antichrist, whereas in Ezekiel 38 these nations attack Israel. However, we have to remember that when this attack occurs, Israel will be living under the protection guaranteed by its covenant with the Antichrist, the leader of the Western confederacy. Thus, any attack against Israel would also be an attack against the Antichrist and his coalition. These two passages are describing the same event, just from two different vantage points.

Also, it's interesting that Ezekiel 38 does not list Egypt among the nations that will invade Israel. Why would Ezekiel fail to mention Egypt if that nation is part of the invading force? I can't answer that question with certainty, but it seems to me that Ezekiel focuses on the outer circle of nations, or the farthest nations in each direction that will come against Israel. It appears to me that other nations inside of that outer ring are also included. If so, Egypt will be one of those nations, according to the parallel passage in Daniel 11:40.

Charles Ryrie describes how the two great end-time power blocs—the king of the North and the king of the South—will unite in a great simultaneous military campaign he calls "the pincer plan":

> A pincer is an instrument with two claws used to grab
> something. Russia, you remember, will want to grab
> Palestine [Israel]. Though she will have six allies, she
> will need one more to form an effective pincer...the
> King of the South is situated perfectly: right on the

southern doorstep of the land that is up for grabs.
Russia will form the northern claw, Egypt the southern claw; put them together—strange alliance that it
will be—and you have the pincer. The attack will be
launched on both fronts simultaneously. The King of
the South will come up from Egypt. The King of the
North will swoop down from Russia, through Turkey
by land and across the Mediterranean by sea...The
target: Palestine [Israel].[20]

Since any attack against Israel will also be an attack against
Antichrist and his Western confederacy, Israel will no doubt
call on him for deliverance from what appears to be certain
annihilation. That's why Daniel 11:40 says, "At the end time
the king of the South will collide with him [the Antichrist],
and the king of the North will storm against him [the Anti-
christ] with chariots, with horsemen and with many ships." As
the Antichrist attempts to come to Israel's defense, something
incredible will occur before he can fire a shot. We know from
Ezekiel 38–39 that this attack on Israel and her ally, the Antichrist, will be supernaturally repelled by God in a dramatic
fashion. God will crush the king of the North and the king
of the South in the land of Israel (Ezekiel 38:18-23). He will
destroy the invaders.

In the aftermath of the destruction, the Antichrist will see
the massive power vacuum that has just been created and will
seize the opportunity to expand his influence. The armies of
all the invaders will have suffered cataclysmic defeat, and as a
result, they will become easy prey to the invading forces of the
Antichrist. Daniel 11:40-43 says,

He will enter countries, overflow them and pass through. He will also enter the Beautiful Land, and many countries will fall; but these will be rescued out of his hand: Edom, Moab and the foremost of the sons of Ammon. Then he will stretch out his hand against other countries, and the land of Egypt will not escape. But he will gain control over the hidden treasures of gold and silver and over all the precious things of Egypt; and Libyans and Ethiopians will follow at his heels. But rumors from the East and from the North will disturb him, and he will go forth with great wrath to destroy and annihilate many.

Several things about this passage are interesting in light of current events. First, this tells us that the first thing the Antichrist will do is secure Israel, and we know from other passages that he will begin his domination of Israel at the point when he breaks his seven-year covenant with Israel at the mid-point of the Tribulation. In the original Hebrew text Daniel 11:41 literally says "and many will fall." Many Jews will die as Antichrist begins his reign of terror.

Second, according to Daniel 11:41, several ancient places will be spared the Antichrist's wrath—namely, Edom, Moab, and Ammon, or modern-day Jordan. Daniel seems to indicate that Jordan will become something of a safe haven or place of refuge for the Jews during this future time of persecution. This may be related to the fact that God will supernaturally protect a remnant of the Jewish people in Jordan during the Tribulation period. In Matthew 24:15-21, Jesus issued this warning to the Jewish people who are alive during the end times:

When you see the ABOMINATION OF DESO-
LATION which was spoken of through Daniel the
prophet, standing in the holy place (let the reader
understand), then those who are in Judea must flee
to the mountains. Whoever is on the housetop must
not go down to get the things out that are in his house.
Whoever is in the field must not turn back to get his
cloak. But woe to those who are pregnant and to those
who are nursing babies in those days! But pray that
your flight will not be in the winter, or on a Sabbath.
For then there will be a great tribulation, such as has
not occurred since the beginning of the world until
now, nor ever will.

Revelation 12:1-17 further details the divine protection by
God of a faithful Jewish remnant in the wilderness during the
final three-and-a-half years of the Tribulation. The Jewish remnant is pictured in that passage as a woman fleeing into the wilderness, pursued by the Antichrist, but supernaturally guided
and guarded by God. Many prophecy teachers believe that
when the Jewish people flee into the wilderness they will be
protected by God in the area of Petra in southern Jordan (see
Micah 2:12, where Bozrah or Petra is a divine place of refuge
for the Jews). Daniel 11:41 supports this idea as well. God will
evidently prepare a city of refuge outside of the Antichrist's
domain for the fleeing remnant. Food, water, and protection
will be miraculously provided. So according to Daniel 11:41,
Jordan will be spared the Antichrist's wrath, but the nations
of North Africa won't fare so well when the Antichrist invades
their territory.

Third, Antichrist will take advantage of this opportunity to chase the remnant of the king of the South back to Egypt, Libya, and Sudan (the Hebrew word is *Cush* and should be translated "Sudan," not "Ethiopia"). Remember that Libya and Cush (Sudan) are two of the nations mentioned in Ezekiel's forecast (Ezekiel 38:5). Daniel 11:40-43 and Ezekiel 38–39 are parallel passages. During his swift foray to the south, the Antichrist will loot, plunder, and seize whatever he can from these defenseless nations in a mop-up operation as he consolidates his power base. He will no doubt take control of the Suez Canal and seize the oil fields of Libya.

Egypt has enjoyed peaceful relations with Israel since 1979, when Prime Minister Menachem Begin and President Anwar Sadat signed the Camp David Accords. But this much we know: Egypt must turn against Israel for Daniel 11:40 to be fulfilled. The day must come when the king of the South will make his move against Israel. What we are witnessing today may be setting the stage for that to occur. We may be seeing the beginning of a major shift. Years ago Henry Kissinger said, "No war in the Middle East is possible without Egypt." [21] The Bible supports that statement. Egypt will be part of the coming Middle East war. What we see taking place today may well be a giant step toward setting up the end-time king of the South.

Egypt in the Millennium

Encyclopedias almost always contain a lengthy section entitled "Ancient Egypt." But isn't it interesting that nowhere do we ever read about future Egypt—except in the Bible? And Scripture has a great deal to say about the coming glory of Egypt. As difficult as it is to envision or believe, the people of

Islamic Egypt will one day be converted and worship the one true God. Nothing could seem more impossible today, but that's exactly what the prophet Isaiah said will happen. Isaiah 19:16-25 takes us all the way to the second coming of Christ at the end of the Tribulation and the final phase of God's plan and purpose for Egypt during the messianic kingdom on earth. Notice the six occurrences of the phrase "in that day" in Isaiah 19:16-25 (vv. 16,18-19,21,23,24). In this context, the phrase places this section of Scripture in the future, in the last days, when Jesus will return to earth to establish His 1000-year messianic kingdom on earth.

> In that day the Egyptians will become like women, and they will tremble and be in dread because of the waving of the hand of the LORD of hosts, which He is going to wave over them. The land of Judah will become a terror to Egypt; everyone to whom it is mentioned will be in dread of it, because of the purpose of the LORD of hosts which He is purposing against them.
>
> In that day five cities in the land of Egypt will be speaking the language of Canaan and swearing allegiance to the LORD of hosts; one will be called the City of Destruction. In that day there will be an altar to the LORD in the midst of the land of Egypt, and a pillar to the LORD near its border. It will become a sign and a witness to the LORD of hosts in the land of Egypt; for they will cry to the LORD because of oppressors, and He will send them a Savior and a Champion, and He will deliver them. Thus the LORD will make Himself

known to Egypt, and the Egyptians will know the LORD in that day. They will even worship with sacrifice and offering, and will make a vow to the LORD and perform it. The LORD will strike Egypt, striking but healing; so they will return to the LORD, and He will respond to them and will heal them.

In that day there will be a highway from Egypt to Assyria, and the Assyrians will come into Egypt and the Egyptians into Assyria, and the Egyptians will worship with the Assyrians.

In that day Israel will be the third party with Egypt and Assyria, a blessing in the midst of the earth, whom the LORD of hosts has blessed, saying, "Blessed is Egypt My people, and Assyria the work of My hands, and Israel My inheritance."

According to Isaiah 19:16-17, Judah will someday control Egypt to such an extent that the Egyptians will live in fear of the Jews. Egypt will recognize Judah as the dominant force in the world. Some maintain this prophecy was fulfilled in 1967 when Israel defeated Egypt in the Six-Day War. However, the following context makes it clear that this still looks to a future time when Christ comes to reign on the earth.

Isaiah 19:18 describes the Egyptians' allegiance to the Lord. Because Egypt has never expressed such an allegiance, clearly this will take place in the future. Evidently, when Israel is the center of Christ's kingdom on earth, the Egyptians will have to learn enough of the Hebrew language to get by. The "City of Destruction," probably better translated "City of the Sun," which is

Heliopolis (dedicated to the worship of the sun god), will turn
to Yahweh. The Egyptians will worship the Lord instead of the
sun god that they worshiped in Isaiah's day, or the moon god,
Allah, which they worship today. This coming transformation
of Eygpt is astounding. As J. Vernon McGee says, "The cross
will yet be the place to which Egypt will look instead of the crescent."[22] Egyptians by the millions will turn to the one true God
for salvation through the cross of Jesus Christ. True worship will
be instituted, and Egypt will openly admit she is worshiping the
God of Israel. This will take place on a nationwide scale.

Then, as a result of the people's proper vertical relationship
with God, a horizontal peace and harmony will exist between
the peoples and nations of the earth. When the hearts of men
are changed, their relationships with others also change. Two
of Israel's age-old enemies and two nations that hated each
other in Isaiah's day—Egypt and Assyria (modern Iraq)—
will be at peace with each other. A superhighway will be constructed from Egypt to Iraq and will pass through Israel so that
people from Egypt and Iraq can worship God together. Israel,
Egypt, and Iraq will have peaceful harmonious relations under
God's hand of blessing.

Imagine these nations as friendly, harmonious neighbors.
Imagine "the United States of Egypt, Israel and Iraq"—with
all the citizens worshiping God together. This will be a stunning development indeed, and given the enmity between these
nations today, the idea that such a peace will ever exist seems
preposterous. As Wilbur Smith said,

> This is the only place in the Old Testament in which
> God assigns to two Gentile nations a place in a trinity

of nations that includes Israel, giving to each a third. Someone has aptly said, here we have the promise of blessing upon the three great divisions of the human race, the Semitic, Japhetic, and Hamitic...The peaceful relationship prevailing among these three nations promised for the end of the age is the very reverse of the conditions now prevailing there.[23]

According to Zechariah 14:16-19, people from Egypt will visit Jerusalem annually to celebrate the Feast of Booths (Tabernacles) with the Jewish people. And if they fail to do so, God will discipline them.

As unlikely as all this seems today, this prophetic promise will be fulfilled just as literally and precisely as all the other prophecies of Scripture that have already come to pass. This will bring the final fulfillment of the Abrahamic Covenant, in which God promised Abraham that "in you all families of the earth will be blessed" (Genesis 12:3). As J. Vernon McGee noted, "Egypt has a glorious future. The nation will enter and enjoy the kingdom with Israel. It may not look like this could be possible in the present hour. Only God can do this."[24] I wholeheartedly agree—only God can do this.

There's a beautiful message here of God's grace to us. Wilbur Smith said, "God's future dealings with Egypt are one of the most beautiful demonstrations of His grace. No nation has as long a history of rejection of divine revelation as Egypt. From the time of Abraham, Joseph and Moses, Egypt has consistently rejected the true God. But in His infinite mercy and grace God will make Himself known to the Egyptians, will bless them and will bring them into harmony with their neighbors."²⁵ This is God's final plan and purpose for Egypt— grace and salvation. What a portrait of God's amazing grace!

Are You Ready?

It's clear that events in our world today bear a remarkable correspondence with the end-time scenario predicted in Scripture. There's a yearning for peace in the Middle East, and globalism is here and growing. The king of the South could be moving into place, which, in turn, means that Christ could come very soon. The next event on God's prophetic calendar is the rapture, when Christ will come to take all His people to heaven. We will be out of here. Then these prophecies about Egypt and many other nations will be literally fulfilled. The central question here is this: Are you ready for the Lord's coming?

I heard a story about a young woman who was expecting her blind date to arrive at 7:00 pm. She was dressed up and ready for his arrival. However, by the time he was an hour late, she figured she'd been stood up. So she removed her makeup, put on her pajamas, gathered up some junk food, and sat down to watch TV with the dog. Just as her favorite show was coming on, the doorbell sounded. She answered the door, and it was her date. He stared at her wide-eyed and said, "I'm two hours late, and you're still not ready?"

Don't be like her. Don't let the lateness of the hour discourage you. Don't give up hope. Be ready when Christ comes! Trust in Him and receive His free gift of eternal life. No one can be saved without receiving Christ. No one is ready without Him. If you have never trusted in Christ, why not accept His grace today? Turn from trusting in yourself and your own good works and trust in Christ alone to be your Savior from sin. Ephesians 2:8-9 says it plainly: "By grace you have been saved through faith; and that not of yourselves, it is the gift of God; not as a result of works, so that no one may boast." Receive His free, full pardon from sin that He purchased for you on the cross!

10 PREDICTIONS ABOUT EGYPT'S FUTURE

1. Egypt will continue to remain an important world power.

2. Egypt and Israel will continue to be hated enemies. The current peace treaty between them must be broken, and that appears to be imminent in light of the recent events taking place in Egypt.

3. Jordan will go it alone, apparently maintaining some degree of neutrality rather than aligning with one of the power blocs. This fits with what we see today, as Jordan has been the least aggressive of Israel's neighbors in recent years.

4. Egypt, the king of the South, will lead a great North African confederacy against Israel during the first half of the Tribulation. This confederacy will include Libya and Sudan. Egypt will also be joined by Russia, the king of the North, in this invasion. Russia will be allied with Turkey and Iran.

5. God will obliterate Egypt's army in Israel.

6. Left defenseless, Egypt will become easy prey for the Antichrist. He will conquer and plunder Egypt, rendering Egypt desolate.

7. Egypt will turn to the Lord for salvation and come to worship the one true God.

8. An altar to the Lord will be built in Egypt, and the people will give sacrifices and offerings to the Lord.

9. A highway will be built between Egypt and Iraq that goes through Israel, and people from Egypt will go up to Jerusalem to celebrate the feasts of the Lord.

10. Egypt will experience a future, national glory that surpasses the greatness it knew in its ancient past.

Chapter 6

Libya's Last Days

Is it the End of Days for Libya?
TIME (FEBRUARY 25, 2011)

After a forty-two year dictatorship and a six-month revolution, the battle finally came to a head and the tyrannical regime of Muammar Gaddafi came crashing down. Like all tyrants, Gaddafi was power-crazed and maniacal, but he took the idea of the mad dictator to a new level. The famous photographer Platon Antoiou recently had a chilling encounter with the Libyan dictator Muammar Gaddafi:

> Three inches from one of the most notorious dictators in history, the photographer Platon focused tightly on the black eyes glaring at him through his lens. "There was nothing in them," he said. "It's like his soul had been scooped out of his head and taken away." The result, a dark and menacing portrait of Libyan leader Muammar Gaddafi…Gaddafi, surrounded by a sea of female bodyguards, approached Platon, who had a small studio set up next to the stage. President Obama had just begun his speech and oddly, Platon said, this

was when Gaddafi wanted to be photographed. "It was scary," Platon says. "He's walking slowly towards me, like some kind of King. It was hellraising…Platon then caught a glimpse of Gaddafi's speech. "It was written in red crayon, in giant letters, like a six-year-old kid would write it. And it was written on about twenty pieces of tatty paper torn out of a book, in Arabic. It felt like notes of a madman."[1]

As Winston Churchill once said about the most famous portrait of himself, "It is not the portrait of a man, but the portrait of a man's soul." The unsettling photo of Gaddafi is the portrait of a tormented soul who has wrecked and ravaged a nation and his own life for more than 40 years. But now, as the old saying goes, the chickens have come home to roost. The domino effect of Arab Spring revolutions reached into Tripoli, eventually unseating Gaddafi and his brutal, cruel grip over Libya. The longest-surviving dictatorship in the region fell suddenly and dramatically, and the news was splashed all over the world:

"The World After Gaddafi" (*Time*, September 5, 2011)

"Rebels Enter Gadhafi's Command Center" (*USA Today*, August 24, 2011)

"Gadhafi's Compound Falls" (*The Wall Street Journal*, August 24, 2011)

"The Liberation of Libya" (*Time*, September, 5, 2001)

"Good Riddance, Gaddafi" (*Newsweek*, September 5, 2011)

"Raving Mad Monster: The modern world has had its deranged panjandrums. But Gaddafi was the finest of them all" (*Newseek*, September 5, 2011)

Who would have ever thought that Libya would be the center of the world's attention for weeks? For months? Yet, that's exactly what happened in 2011 as rebellion erupted, the stalemate ensued, and finally the madman was deposed, then killed. A *Time* article appropriately titled "Gaddafi's Last Stand" noted,

> Leave it to Libya's Muammar Gaddafi to show the world how a tyrant goes down: with bluster, belligerence and blood. Not for him, the quiet escape of Tunisia's Zine el Abidine Ben Ali or the noisy—but broadly peaceful—exit of Egypt's Hosni Mubarak. When the Arab youth uprising that has toppled despots on either side of his North African nation arrived on his doorstep, Gaddafi gave notice that the region's longest-surviving dictatorship would not succumb to revolutionary rap songs, Facebook pages and nonviolent demonstrations; he dispatched tanks and jet fighters to pound and strafe protesters. Hundreds were killed—the exact toll is impossible to know, since the regime shut out the world's media and shut down most communications.[2]

The world focus on Libya is captivating from the geopolitical perspective, and is especially important in light of Ezekiel 38:5, which predicts that Libya (ancient *Put* or *Phut*) will be part of an end-time confederacy of nations that will come against Israel in the last days. The presence of Libya on 24/7 news coverage is interesting to say the least. It fits what we should expect if the Gog coalition is drawing near.

Before we look in more detail at what is transpiring in Libya today and how it appears to be setting the stage for end-time events, let's gain a little historical and political background first.

Learning about Libya

Here's a brief thumbnail sketch of Libya today:

> Libya is a sea of sand, but beneath that sand is oil. Libya is about the size of Alaska and Oregon combined...Summer temperatures rise to a blistering 130 degrees in the shade. Choking dust storms frequently obliterate the landscape. When Libya gained its independence after World War II, there were only sixteen college graduates in the country; per capita income averaged about thirty dollars a year.[3]

Knowing this, one might legitimately ask, "Why does anyone care about Libya?" The answer is quite simple and pragmatic: Libya is positioned on the North African coast just across the Mediterranean Sea from vital NATO nations of Europe. Also, Libya is rich in oil. The nation is a member of OPEC and pumps about 1.6 million barrels of oil a day. Libya has the world's ninth largest-known oil deposits and just over 6.5 million people. It is the seventeenth largest producer of oil in the world and the third largest in Africa. The lion's share of its production goes to Europe (85 percent), with the rest shipped to Asia.

After gaining its independence, Libya had its own king from 1951 to 1968. But that all changed suddenly in 1969 when Muammar Gaddafi (also spelled Qaddafi), at barely 27 years of age, seized power and deposed King Idris in a bloodless coup. Gaddafi was inspired by Egypt's President Gamal Abdel Nasser:

> In September 1968 the Libyan king was deposed by a group of army officers led by a belligerent and unstable Bedouin named Muammar al-Qaddafi. Qaddafi, born in a goatskin tent in the Sahara, came from a tribe of nomads who stopped occasionally to scratch a meager crop from the reluctant soil before moving on again with their herds. Qaddafi idolized Egypt's Colonel Nasser, who had helped rid Egypt of King Farouk and turn the country into a republic. Qaddafi decided that the army offered the quickest way to power, so he enrolled in the Libyan Royal Academy. He wasted no time in organizing his fellow cadets into a group modeled on the one that brought Nasser to power in Egypt. Qaddafi bided his time; then, when the aged King Idris was vacationing in Greece, Qaddafi and his friends seized power. One of his first acts...was to turn the social calendar back to the thirteenth century. Alcohol was banned, mixed dancing was prohibited, and women, because of their "biological defects," were told to stay at home. He also took Libya on a new political course. He ordered Americans out of the strategic air base on the outskirts of Tripoli, nationalized foreign-owned businesses without compensation, and redirected the flow of the country's growing oil

revenues. He invested in hospitals, roads, houses, irrigation projects—and international terrorism...One of Qaddafi's dreams has been to create a federation with other Arab states...Qaddafi violently opposed Sadat's attempts to make peace with Israel. He vehemently rejected peace with Israel, recognition of Israel and negotiations with Israel.[4]

In 1973 Gaddafi declared a "cultural revolution" and imposed sharia law on the people of Libya. President Ronald Reagan aptly called him the "mad dog of the Middle East" in a speech given on April 9, 1986. Reagan then imposed sanctions against Libya and launched air strikes against Tripoli and Benghazi in retaliation for a Libyan terrorist attack against a Berlin disco that killed 40 Americans. The raid struck strategic targets and even Gaddafi's home. He escaped, but one of his sons was killed. In 1988, after Pan-Am Flight 103 blew up in the air over Lockerbie, Scotland, investigations eventually traced the culprits to Libya, which has served for decades as a hub and haven for bloodthirsty terrorists.

It's All Still About Israel

One evening in March 2011 I was watching CNN coverage of the revolt in Libya, and a reporter who was on the ground with the anti-government forces (or rebels) gave his view on the motivation behind the uprising. He said he had talked with hundreds of rebel forces, and incredibly, he went on to say that "one out of five told me that they were fighting Gaddafi because they believe he is part Jewish." This was a wake-up call to me that there were all kinds of reasons behind the rebellion. This didn't involve some homogeneous group of "freedom fighters" who were seeking liberation and democracy. At least 20 percent of them wanted to kill Gaddafi because, according to this reporter, they believed they have Jewish blood coursing through their veins. This response was understandable given the fact Gaddafi had vowed to destroy Israel on numerous occasions. Given Gaddafi's anti-Semitism, it's clear that Libya is a natural fit with the other nations listed in Ezekiel 38 who will descend upon Israel in the end times.

Libya in the Bible

What does the Bible tell us about Libya? Libya is referred to numerous times, both directly and indirectly.

- *Matthew 27:32*—A man from Libya, Simon of Cyrene (a part of ancient Libya), carried the cross for our Lord Jesus.

- *Acts 2:10*—It is clear that Jews from Libya were present in Jerusalem on the Day of Pentecost and heard the apostle Peter preach the gospel in the power of the Holy Spirit. About 3000 people turned to Jesus Christ that day and trusted in Him for salvation. Libyans were among them, since they are mentioned in the text.

- *Acts 11:20*—Libyan (Cyrenean) followers of Jesus Christ helped bring the gospel to Antioch and Syria, and led people to Christ.

- *Acts 13:1*—A man from Libya—Lucius of Cyrene—became one of the leaders of the church

at Antioch, sending out Barnabas and Paul to take
the gospel to Asia.

This evidence should be enough to convince us that the Lord
loves the people of Libya. He wants them to know Him and
receive His free gift of salvation. We should pray for Libya and
other Middle Eastern and North African nations that many
there will turn to Christ alone for their salvation before He
comes. That should be our attitude toward all nations in this
present age.

Libya's Future

There are two main Old Testament passages that fore-
tell the future of Libya. The first is Ezekiel 38:5, which lists
ancient *Put* as a participant in the end-time Gog alliance that
will invade Israel. As we have already seen, *Put* or *Phut*, in
Ezekiel's day, was the land to the west of Egypt and certainly
includes Libya but could also encompass modern-day Algeria
and Tunisia, two other nations that have experienced the so-
called Arab awakening.

The second passage that relates Libya's last days is one we
examined when we considered the future of Egypt, Daniel
11:40-45:

> At the end time the king of the South will collide with
> him, and the king of the North will storm against him
> with chariots, with horsemen and with many ships;
> and he will enter countries, overflow them and pass
> through. He will also enter the Beautiful Land, and
> many countries will fall; but these will be rescued out

of his hand: Edom, Moab and the foremost of the sons of Ammon. Then he will stretch out his hand against other countries, and the land of Egypt will not escape. But he will gain control over the hidden treasures of gold and silver and over all the precious things of Egypt; and Libyans and Ethiopians will follow at his heels. But rumors from the East and from the North will disturb him, and he will go forth with great wrath to destroy and annihilate many. He will pitch the tents of his royal pavilion between the seas and the beautiful Holy Mountain; yet he will come to his end, and no one will help him.

As already stated in the previous chapter, I believe Daniel 11:40-43 parallels Ezekiel 38–39. After the Gog alliance, which includes Libya, rises up against Israel, the Antichrist will invade Israel, break his covenant with her, and then will make his foray into North Africa in a mop-up operation to further consolidate his power. One of the nations he will subdue is Libya. With its army decimated on the mountains of Israel by the hand of God (Ezekiel 38:19-23), Libya will be helpless against the Antichrist's advances and will fall into his hands, becoming yet another nation under the Antichrist's growing umbrella of influence that will eventually encompass the entire world.

Events we are witnessing today in Libya and many other nations appear to be paving the way for the fulfillment of these ancient prophecies. Libya is front and center in the world headlines. Several of the nations that will be part of the Gog coalition have had a part in helping the Libyan rebels toward victory.

Turkey provided Libyan rebels with over $200 million, while Iran also cheered and aided them.

But what is next? Much more is at stake than just getting rid of another brutal autocrat—that's usually the easy part. The larger battle is building a stable nation. Translating a military victory into building a country is a daunting task. The big question is this: What will a post-Gaddafi Libya look like? Some believe that Libya can become a democratic, stable nation. For the sake of the Libyan people, I hope this is true. No one wants to see further chaos and suffering there. But those who believe Libya will take this route are in the minority. Dirk Vandewalle, who takes a more neutral wait-and-see posture, observes "there are two daunting challenges. The first is state-building: the creation and maintenance of the most basic civil institutions...In the aftermath of the civil war, state building will begin from scratch. The second challenge will be to turn Libya into a unified nation for the first time in its history."[5] Everyone agrees that those are the two central problems faced by the transition council, but most experts forecast a much darker future.

Some warn that Libya could easily descend into chaos and become fertile soil for Islamic terror. David Mack, a former Deputy Assistant Secretary of State for Near East Affairs, told *Time* that the worst possible outcome would be a widespread chaos and lawlessness in which Libya degenerated into a kind of "Somalia on the Mediterranean."[6] That would be a nightmare scenario for the United States and Israel, for then Libya would become a dreaded magnet and haven for the worst elements in the world of terrorism. Niall Ferguson said,

> Since the beginning of the Arab revolutions more
> than six months ago, I have repeatedly warned that
> the chances of a happily-ever-after ending are much
> lower than the chances of escalating violence across the
> region. Coming soon: the rebel factions in Libya get
> down to the serious business of fighting...each other.[7]

In the wake of the revolution, there are growing fears that radical elements "are part of an Islamist fifth column preparing to make a power grab in the new Libya."[8] One of the most effective commanders among the anti-Gaddafi forces in Libya fought in Afghanistan against the Soviets and alongside al-Qaeda in the dying days of the Taliban regime. Then he went on to serve as commander of the anti-Gaddafi forces in Tripoli. He claims that he is just an ordinary Libyan fighting for freedom, but many are not quick to believe him. Fears of an Islamist takeover are real.

What shape will the post-Gaddafi Libya take? Will there be civil war among the various factions? Will Islamists come out on top? Will the nation descend into the kind of chaos like that found in Somalia? No one knows for sure, but if any of these scenarios were to emerge, or even some combination of them, Libya would be ripe for membership in the Gog coalition. Under Gaddafi, Libya had been prepared for Ezekiel's prophesied war of the end times. As John Phillips observes, "There will almost certainly be some ebb and flow in the events connected with Libya. But Ezekiel has no doubts; Libya will join with Russia as an enthusiastic member of the anti-Israel coalition."[9]

After that, according to the prophet Daniel, Libya will

come under the iron-fisted control and direction of the Antichrist. That's what Scripture reveals about Libya's future. What we see in today's headlines strikingly foreshadows what the prophets predicted over 2500 years ago. Events are quickly falling in line. The signposts on the road to the end times are in full view. Yet we know that God loves those who live in Libya, and that we should pray for their salvation before it's too late.

Chapter 7

Northern Storm: Russia, Turkey, and Iran

*In the thirty-eighth chapter of Ezekiel it says God will take
the children of Israel from among the heathen [where]
they'd been scattered and will gather them again in the
promised land. Ezekiel says that...the nation that will
lead all the other powers into darkness against Israel will
come out of the north. What other powerful nation is to the
north of Israel [besides Russia]? None. But it didn't seem
to make sense before the Russian revolution, when Russia
was a Christian country. Now it does, now that Russia has
become communistic and atheistic, now that Russia has set
itself against God. Now it fits the description perfectly.*[1]

PRESIDENT RONALD REAGAN

he battle of Gog and Magog, the coming Middle East
war, will involve many different nations. Over 2500 years
ago, the prophet Ezekiel went so far as to name the precise geographical entities—all of whom are identifiable nations
today—that will one day attack Israel. Several of these countries are to the north of Israel, and as we have already seen,
they will form a confederacy with "the king of the North." It
appears this king of the North will rise at the same time we
see events shaping up for the kings of the South and the West.

Earlier, in chapter 3, we identified the northern nations in Eze-kiel 38 as Russia, the Central Asia nations that were formerly part of the Soviet Union, Iran, and Turkey. Let's consider how this "northern storm" is coming together.

The Northern Confederacy

Tracking the Bear

One of the most significant international developments in the last 50 years, one that is a necessary prerequisite for the Eze-kiel 38–39 invasion, is the remarkable rise of Russia to a place of world prominence. Along with the United States, Russia (previously the Soviet Union) has been a world military super-power. Although some hopeful signs of democracy appeared in Russia after the dissolution of the Soviet Union in 1991, Rus-sia today is rapidly regressing back to her old totalitarian, auto-cratic ways.[2] She has a vital interest in the Middle East and Persian Gulf; this is her neighborhood. Some control over this area is vital to Russia's national security. Moreover, since the fall of the Soviet empire, the great Russian bear has been like a mother bear robbed of her cubs. The fall of her empire brought national humiliation. Russia seems to long for the good old days of the USSR, and the president of Russia is looking more and more like a modern czar.

Russia is establishing and deepening its ties to the other nations listed in Ezekiel 38:1-6. It has spread its influence in the five mostly Muslim nations that used to form the under-belly of the Soviet Union. These five nations, which occupy the land of ancient Magog, are often called the "stans" because their names all end with *stan*, which means "nation" or "land."

These nations are Tajikistan, Uzbekistan, Kazakhstan, Turkmenistan, and Kyrgyzstan. Russia is moving aggressively to extend its influence throughout the former Soviet empire.

Russia has also made relations with Iran a top priority. After the controversial elections in Iran in June 2010, in which Mahmoud Ahmadinejad returned to office, the first place Ahmadinejad entreated for support was Moscow.

Russia continues to cozy up to Iran, helping Iran construct its nuclear reactors and providing nuclear fuel. While Syria is not specifically mentioned in Ezekiel 38, Russia is considering helping Syria build nuclear reactors as well. Russia is also deepening its ties with Turkey. In May 2010, "Turkey and Russia signed 17 agreements…to enhance cooperation in energy and other fields, including pacts to build Turkey's first nuclear power plant and furthering plans for an oil pipeline from the Black Sea to the Mediterranean. The pipeline would allow Russia to expand its oil exports from the Black Sea, bypassing the Bosporus, whose shipping lines are already at capacity."[3] President Medvedev of Russia hopes that trade with Turkey will soon reach $30 billion and will ultimately top $100 billion.

Concerning Russia and the northern alliance, God says in Ezekiel 38:4, "I will turn you about and put hooks into your jaws, and I will bring you out." Many have often wondered about these "hooks" God will use to draw Russia into the battle of Gog and Magog. While no one can know for sure, it could be that Russia's alliances with all these Muslim nations will be the "magnetic force" God will use in the end times to pull them into Israel to meet their doom. For Russia, the opportunity to lead an Islamic coalition in an invasion of Israel would serve as a chance for her to reclaim her lost glory, elevate her status with her Islamic neighbors, and assert control over the Middle East. Whatever means God uses, it's clear from Scripture that the tracks of the Russian bear will lead straight to the land of Israel, and that the connections between Russia and her Islamic neighbors are consistent with what Scripture prophesies.

Let's Talk Turkey

A couple decades ago, any talk of Turkey being a regional power or superpower would have sounded absurd, but in recent years, all that has changed dramatically. The Turkish phoenix is rising. Ninety years after the fall of the Ottoman Empire, Turkey is rousing itself from isolation to become a major player in the new Middle East. Turkey's economy is white hot. It was the second-fastest-growing economy in the world in 2010. Politically, Turkey is being looked to by other Muslim nations as a model. "The dramatic toppling of dictatorships in the Middle East has launched a new era and a quest for democratic vision in the Muslim world. As the international community anxiously anticipates the outcomes of uprisings in Tunisia, Libya, Egypt, and the Gulf states, Turkey has maneuvered itself into the spotlight."[4] Turkish foreign minister Ahmet Davutoglu said, "If the world is on fire, Turkey is the firefighter. Turkey is assuming the leading role for stability in the Middle East."[5]

According to Hillel Fradkin and Lewis Libby, Turkish prime minister Recep Tayyip Erdogan is pushing forcefully "to be viewed not merely as *a* leader in the Muslim world, but *the* leader."[6] The concern is that at the same time Turkey is gaining more influence, its relations with the West and Israel are deteriorating rapidly. As *Newsweek* reported,

> Turkey, says the conventional wisdom, is "turning east." Over the last two years Prime Minister Recep Tayyip Erdogan has proclaimed Iranian President Mahmoud Ahmadinejad a "good friend" and blasted Israel for attacking a Turkish aid convoy to Gaza. He signed accords with Syria and Iraq and defended Sudanese President Omar al-Bashir as "a good Muslim."...Foreign Minister Ahmet Davutoglu caused outrage in Israel by meeting with Hamas leader Khaled Meshaal.[7]

These alliances with Iran and Sudan point toward Ezekiel 38, which mentions both of those nations.

The new posture in Turkey is not an encouraging sign for Israel or the US. The 2011 Gaza flotilla incident, which resulted in the deaths of nine Turkish citizens, pushed Turkey into a leading role as an anti-Israel instigator. Anti-Semitism and anti-Israel sentiment is sharply on the increase in Turkey. In a dramatic move in September 2011, Turkey expelled Israel's ambassador and severed all military ties with Israel. There are growing concerns that Egypt and Jordan will follow Turkey's lead.[8]

The climate in Turkey began to shift in 2002 when the AKP (Turkish Justice and Development Party) was swept to power in a landslide victory. This party has exercised increasing influence in the country, turning Turkey from a secular nation to an Islamist one. Turkey has been a secular democratic state

since the fall of the Ottoman Empire and the establishment
of the Republic of Turkey in 1923 by its revered leader Mus-
tafa Kemal Atatürk. However, "since the rise to power of the
Islamist AKP in 2002, Prime Minister Erdogan has cleverly
and gradually tilted the country eastward, muzzled the press,
and diminished the military's role."[9]

An article in *World* magazine sounded this alarm over Turkey's growing influence:

> Turkey is becoming a model to many in a transition-
> ing Middle East—but that may not be as encourag-
> ing as it seems...Touting Turkey's growing leadership
> on the chessboard of regional geopolitics and success
> in creating a model Muslim democracy, Ankara (and
> its growing number of fans in the Middle East) claims
> it can serve as a beacon to Arab countries in transition.
> But the erosion of democratic freedoms at home calls
> into question Turkey's ultimate direction and raises
> concerns about a country that is becoming increas-
> ingly Islamist and gradually more powerful.[10]

Some believe that a rewriting of the Turkish Constitution,
which would give the prime minister greater powers, could be
in the offing.

Turkey is forging alliances with its neighbors, many of
whom are specifically mentioned in Ezekiel 38. Turkish president Abdullah Gul has visited Egypt and met with Iranian
president Mahmoud Ahmadinejad while Turkish prime minister Recep Tayyip Erdogan has held talks with Syrian president Bashar al-Assad. Even before the Arab revolutions broke

out, Turkey was already busily jockeying for regional prestige by forging alliances with Iran, Libya, and Syria. Turkey has consistently sided with Iran in its controversial nuclear program and against US-sponsored sanctions against Iran. Turkey bankrolled the Libyan rebels in their uprising against the Gaddafi regime, providing them with $200 million.[11]

A *Newsweek* article about Turkish prime minister Erdogan was titled "Eastern Star" in recognition of his desire to turn Turkey to the east:

> The fear is that the prime minister could turn away from Turkey's traditional Western alliances and join forces instead with anti-U.S. hardliners in the Middle East. Recently, the nervousness has become more palpable than ever. First, Erdogan teamed up with President Luiz Inácio Lula da Silva of Brazil in an effort to block U.N. sanctions against Iran's nuclear program. And then Erdogan accused Israel of "state-sponsored terrorism" and broke off military ties after an Israeli commando raid on a Turkish flotilla that was carrying aid to Gaza. Turkey has long been America's closest Muslim ally, and its formula for separating mosque and state in a thriving democracy seemed a model for the rest of the region…What worries Turkey's Western allies most, though, is Erdogan's chumminess with the likes of Mahmoud Ahmadinejad. Scenes of Erdogan embracing the Iranian president this May and calling him "my good friend" drove the White House wild…On a gut level, Erdogan feels "more comfortable in Tehran or Moscow than Brussels or

Washington," says Ian Lesser of the German Marshall Fund of the United States…That stance, combined with Erdogan's fiery remarks about Turkey's former ally Israel—calling Gaza a "prison camp" and denying that Hamas is a terrorist organization—have made him a hero to many Arabs.[12]

When the United States reduces its presence in the Middle East there are three scenarios that Western experts especially fear: civil war, Islamic revolution, and/or a revived Ottoman Empire led by Turkey. A revived Ottoman Empire appeared very unlikely in recent years because Turkey was leaning westward as the founder of the republic, Kemal Ataturk, had intended. Turkey was aggressively vying to become part of the European Union. But that all changed dramatically in 2003 with the election of Erdogan as prime minister. In June 2011, he was elected to a third term. Niall Ferguson observes:

> Since 2003, when Recep Tayyip Erdogan was elected prime minister, that has changed. The founder of the Justice and Development Party (AKP), Erdogan is a seductive figure. To many, he is the personification of moderate Islamism…And yet we need to look more closely at Erdogan. For there is good reason to suspect he dreams of transforming Turkey in ways Suleiman the Magnificent would have admired…This explains his sustained campaign to alter the Turkish Constitution in ways that would increase his own power at the expense of the judiciary and the press as well as the military, all bastions of secularism. It explains his

increasingly strident criticism of Israel's "state terror-ism" in Gaza.[13]

When Erdogan was mayor in Istanbul, he was imprisoned for publicly reciting some lines from a Turkish poet: "The mosques are our barracks, the domes our helmets, the min-arets our bayonets, and the faithful our soldiers."[14] He clearly wants to return to the days when Turkey was militantly Mus-lim and a regional superpower. This fits what the Bible predicts in Ezekiel 38 to a T. Could *Wall Street Journal* editorialist Rob-ert L. Pollock be right when he warns that Erdogan is leading the country on "a national decline into madness"?[15]

There is growing concern that Turkey, like the other Arab nations, will experience an erosion of democratic freedoms and a corresponding strengthening of Islamist government rule. If Turkey is the model for the Middle East, a Turkish slide into an Islamist dictatorship could be the first of many dominos to fall. When he was mayor of Istanbul, current Turkish prime minis-ter Erdogan made this chilling statement: "Democracy is like a streetcar. You ride it until you get to your destination and then you get off."[16] Is the Turkish streetcar of democracy about to reach its destination? Might we see an "Arab fall" or "Arab win-ter" in Turkey? Could events in Turkey be paving the way for it to play a part in the coming northern storm? No one knows what twists and turns may lie ahead, but Scripture clearly indi-cates Turkey will be a part of the end-time Gog confederacy. All the signs are pointing in the same direction.

Iran Rising

One hardly needs to describe the situation in Iran today and how it corresponds with Ezekiel's prophecy. Since the Islamic revolution in 1979 and the formation of the Islamic Republic of Iran, the Iranian mullah regime has led the nation in a deepening death spiral. Current president Mahmoud Ahmadinejad regularly spews out venom against Israel and denies the Holocaust, while in a tragic irony, works feverishly to repeat it. Infamous for his anti-Zionist statements, Ahmadinejad said in April 2011 that "a new Middle East will emerge without the presence of the United States and the Zionist regime [Israel], and their allies in the near future."[17] He has threatened repeatedly that, "anybody who recognizes Israel will burn in the fire of the Islamic nation's fury."[18] At a celebration of Army Day he blamed the US for the unrest in the Middle East and for working to create division between Shia and Sunni Muslims, saying, "The era of Zionism and capitalism has passed away." He also leveled threats against Saudi Arabia and other more moderate Gulf States.[19]

Behind all the rhetoric lies a mystical Islamic theology that sees current events in the Middle East preparing the way for the coming of the Madhi, or messiah. Within Shiite Islam, which dominates Iran, an Imam is a spiritual leader who is allegedly a bloodline relative of the prophet Muhammad. There is a prophecy in Islam about the coming of the twelfth Imam—Imam Muhammad Abul Qasim. It's believed by the Twelver sect that he disappeared in AD 878 in the cave of the great mosque of Samarra without leaving any descendants. It's also taught that the twelfth Imam was still active and communicated with by messengers until AD 941, when all communication and contact with this world was cut off. According to Islamic teaching, he will return near the end of the world. Their end-time view says that when he returns, he will rule the earth for seven years, bringing about final judgment and end of the world.

Anton La Guardia makes this chilling observation about Ahmadinejad's "apocalypse now" theology:

> After a cataclysmic confrontation with evil and darkness, the Mahdi will lead the world to an era of universal peace…Indeed, the Hidden Imam is expected to return in the company of Jesus. Mr. Ahmadinejad appears to believe that these events are close at hand and that ordinary mortals can influence the divine timetable. The prospect of such a man obtaining nuclear weapons is worrying. The unspoken question is this: is Mr. Ahmadinejad now tempting a clash with the West because he feels safe in the belief of the imminent return of the Hidden Imam? Worse, might he be trying to provoke chaos in the hope of hastening his reappearance?[20]

Ahmadinejad firmly believes that the Mahdi controls events in Iran and around the world, and that things are shaping up quickly for his coming. In 2008 he said,

> The Imam Mahdi is in charge of the world and we see his hand directing all the affairs of the country. We must solve Iran's internal problems *as quickly as possible. Time is lacking.* A movement has started for us to occupy ourselves with our global responsibilities, which are *arriving with great speed.* Iran will be the

focal point of the management of the world, thanks to God. In this region an event has to happen. The hand of God must appear and will make the roots of injustice in the world vanish. [21]

Ahmadinejad believes an end-time war will sweep the Mahdi to power. In a sense, then, Iran's participation in the Ezekiel 38 war could be viewed as a self-fulfilling prophecy.

SHOW ME THE MAHDI

Fast Facts about the Mahdi

- Won't come in an odd-numbered year (Islamic calendar)
- Will appear in Mecca
- Will travel from Mecca to Kufa (Iraq)
- 40 years old at time of emergence
- Will remove all injustice and bring universal prosperity
- Jesus will return with him and be his deputy
- Will wear a ring that belonged to King Solomon
- Will carry wooden staff of Moses
- Will rule for seven years

Iran is elated about all the uprisings across the Middle East except the one in its close ally, Syria. The Iranians view these revolts as a sign of the Mahdi's soon coming and an open door to expand their influence. Former US ambassador at the UN, John Bolton, has been a vigilant watchdog of Iran's regional and nuclear pursuits. He points out how Iran is seizing the unrest in the Middle East to foster its own purposes:

> I think Iran is currently taking advantage of the turmoil in the Middle East to advance its own hegemonic aspirations in the region. It's clearly interfered in the situation in Bahrain and it would like to interfere in Saudi Arabia. I think the real essence of the problem long-term is Iran's continuing support for terrorism, its continuing pursuit of nuclear weapons. As we focus on Libya or Egypt or other headlines of the day, we shouldn't lose sight that the great conflict, the great risk, is an expansive Iran.[22]

Joel Rosenberg agrees:

> The leaders in Tehran could not be more excited by the revolution now underway in Egypt and are praying the Mubarak regime collapses and the Muslim Brotherhood come to power. For them, such events would be dramatic new evidence that the End of Days has come, infidel Arab regimes are on the road to collapse, Western influence in the Mideast is declining, Israel is one step closer to being annihilated, and the Twelfth Imam is one step closer to arriving and establishing the worldwide Islamic kingdom known as the "caliphate."[23]

In 2011 a movie called *The Coming Is Near* was released in Iran. It is an eerie "second coming" propaganda video. It was distributed throughout the region to announce the soon arrival of the Mahdi and "instigate further uprisings in Arab countries."[24] Here are some quotes and statements about the movie:[25]

- "Iran will soon usher in the end times."

- "The Iranian regime believes the chaos is divine proof that their ultimate victory is at hand."

- "It describes current events in the Middle East as a prelude to the arrival of the mythical twelfth Imam or Mahdi—the messiah figure who Islamic scriptures say will lead the armies of Islam to victory over all non-Muslims in the last days."

- "The video claims that Iran is destined to rise as a great power in the last days to help defeat America and Israel and usher in the return of the Mahdi. And it makes clear the Iranians believe that time is fast approaching."

- The video describes Ahmadinejad and Iran's Supreme Ayatollah Khamenei as the leaders who will bring about Mahdi's return. It condemns the United States and Israel, and offers praise to the Muslim Brotherhood for helping to overthrow the government of Hosni Mubarak in Egypt.

Jonathon M. Seidl further describes this propaganda piece:

The Hadith have clearly described the events and the various transformations of countries in the Middle East and also that of Iran in the age of the coming, said a narrator, who went on to say that America's invasion of Iraq was foretold by Islamic scripture— and that the Mahdi will one day soon rule the world from Iraq. The ongoing upheavals in other Middle

Eastern countries like Yemen and Egypt—including the rise of the Muslim Brotherhood—are also analyzed as prophetic signs that the Mahdi is near—so is the current poor health of the king of Saudi Arabia, an Iranian rival...Iran's supreme leader, Ayatollah Khamenei, and Hassan Nasrallah, leader of Iran's terrorist proxy Hezbollah, are hailed as pivotal end times players, whose rise was predicted in Islamic scripture. The same goes for Iran's President Mahmoud Ahmadinejad, who the video says will conquer Jerusalem prior to the Mahdi's coming. [26]

Here's a quote from the movie:

Therefore let us shout out loud that The Coming is soon and that evil should be fearful. We live with these thoughts every day and our lives are filled with The Coming of the last Imam. That human will reappear and fill the world with justice and establish his promised governance on earth. The very world has witnessed too much bloodshed of the innocent for others to build their palaces. The very world is filled with shouts for justice. The innocent and the oppressed are losing their lives to world powers. It is in this very world where the oppressors rule and this world that Allah will command the last Imam to appear and forever put an end to injustice. At that time, the world will belong to the righteous. [27]

Everything we see today suggests that Iran is on a collision course with Israel and the United States and would gladly join with the Gog alliance when it comes together. There's also a sizable rift between Iran and the Sunni-dominated Arab nations, such as Saudi Arabia and the Gulf States. This corresponds to the picture presented in Ezekiel 38–39. In that prophecy, as Russia, Central Asia, Iran, Turkey, North Sudan, and Libya (and possibly other nations) join together to assault Israel, a group of other nations sit on the sidelines offering a lame protest to what's happening. The nations that are named—Sheba and Dedan—are now known as Saudi Arabia and the more moderate Gulf States.

Arab Spring or Nuclear Winter?
What If Israel Hit Iran's Nuclear Sites?

I've heard Joel Rosenberg say that Israeli prime minister Benjamin Netanyahu told him that he believes he was put on earth to stop the next holocaust. The nation most likely to try and make a holocaust a reality, however, is Iran. Iran's mullah regime is working feverishly and fiendishly to cross the nuclear finish line, and one would have to be supremely naïve not to believe that the target in the crosshairs is Israel. For this reason, Israel is doing all it can to stall or temporarily cripple Iran's nuclear aspirations.

In 2010, a computer virus or worm called Stuxnet hit the computer systems used in Iran's nuclear program. The precise source of the virus is still unknown, but most believe Israel was behind it, and possibly the United States. While the full effects of this virus are still not known for certain, initial reports estimate it may have set Iran's nuclear program back as much as two years. There have been hazy reports of other suspected viruses as well.

Whatever the case, we can be sure that Israel and the United States are working clandestinely to do all they can to thwart Iran's atomic ambitions. Israel is cautiously watching and waiting for the point of no return—the moment when Iran has crossed the nuclear finish line and has everything necessary to make a deliverable nuclear weapon. When Israeli intelligence is convinced that Iran has reached that point, Israel will feel compelled to make a preemptive attack. The nation will have no other choice. But doing that could easily trigger a crushing response from Iran and its surrogates Hezbollah, Hamas, and Syria. At a meeting in Davos, Switzerland, in late January 2011, "A diverse panel of decision-makers and experts from the United States, Europe and the Middle East found common ground on just one thing when it comes to dealing with the Iranian nuclear program: A military strike could well spark a devastating counterattack."[28]

If Israel were to use precision nuclear strikes to take out the Iranian nuclear megaplex, that would plant seeds of vitriolic hatred against Israel in Iran and much of the Muslim world. That, in turn, could easily precipitate the Gog invasion in the very near future. Such events could serve as the explosive catalyst for many Muslim nations to begin a plot for an all-out attack, a final payback, against Israel, and could even be the "hooks" in the "jaws" that draws Russia into the fray. General Jerry Boykin, a retired three-star general and former undersecretary of defense for intelligence, said, "If Israel were to strike Iran…you would see it accelerate the relationship between Russia and Iran. I think Russia would then come to the aid of…the Iranians and I think you would see that relationship solidify with increased military cooperation and military support, the sale of additional military equipment and even military advice. And that sets the stage for ultimately what is described in Ezekiel 38 and 39."[29]

Things are clearly in a state of flux right now, but the Bible is clear about what will ultimately transpire.

Coincidence or Providence?

The Russian bear has roared out of hibernation and is back on the prowl in the Middle East. Russia has its hands in every aspect of Middle East politics and is cozying up to Iran, Turkey, and the nations of Central Asia that were formerly part of the Soviet Union. Since the Islamic revolution in 1979, Iran has burst on the world scene as the world's greatest state sponsor of terror and threat to international stability. Its Mahdi theology and the belief that it can hasten his coming pours rocket fuel upon the spreading fires in the Middle East. And Turkey is clearly "moving east," just as we should expect if the battle of Gog and Magog is on the horizon. Turkey is forging alliances with Iran, Russia, Libya, and Sudan—four of the other nations listed in Ezekiel 38.

Is it mere coincidence that the northern storm is coalescing, or is it mighty providence? Are Russia, Turkey, and Iran ascending and becoming allies with one another by sheer chance? The answer seems clear: The sovereign God of prophecy is orchestrating world events to bring about His sovereign purposes in His time. Current events point toward the fulfillment of the Gog prophecy and the emerging of the northern storm:

- Israel has been regathered to her homeland.

- The world is desperate for peace in the Middle East.

- All the nations in Ezekiel 38 are identifiable entities in existence today with the will and desire to attack Israel.

- The nations in Ezekiel 38 are presently forming alliances with one another.

- An Israeli strike against Iran's nuclear facilities could serve as the catalyst that brings about the rise of the northern storm against Israel.

We have looked at what Scripture says about many of the nations surrounding Israel and how current events dovetail with the scriptural predictions about those nations. But what about the nations we haven't considered yet—nations like Syria, Lebanon, and others? Does the Bible mention anything about them in relation to the end times? That's where we'll turn our attention in the next two chapters.

Chapter 8

What About the Psalm 83 War?

*Behold, Your enemies make an uproar, and those who hate
You have exalted themselves. They make shrewd plans against
Your people, and conspire together against Your treasured
ones. They have said, "Come, and let us wipe them out as a
nation, that the name of Israel be remembered no more."*

PSALM 83:2-4

In the summer of 2006, when Israel was under brutal, sustained assault by Hezbollah from the north and Hamas from the west, a 1000-year-old book of Psalms was discovered by a construction worker in a bog in Ireland. *National Geographic* described the find: "About 20 pages long and written in Latin, the book has been dated to between A.D. 800 and 1000. It is the first early medieval text to be discovered in Ireland in 200 years, the archaeologists say."[1]

What I found interesting is that, according to *National Geographic*, "the book was found open, perhaps rather portentously, to Psalm 83, in which God hears of nations' attempts to wipe out the name of Israel."[2] Many saw this as some kind of sign that God was about to deal with the enemies of Israel and bring this ancient psalm to fulfillment. Of course, the fulfillment of Psalm 83 did not occur in 2006 as some expected.

But recently, there has been a renewed focus on Psalm 83 as a prophecy that will likely be fulfilled in the near future.

Over the past couple years I have been asked quite regularly, both in person and by email, about Psalm 83 and the war it describes. These questions come up at every prophecy conference I attend or speak at. Until now I have never addressed the Psalm 83 war in writing, but I have spent quite a bit of time thinking about it. I believe that in light of the current mayhem in the Middle East, it's appropriate for us to take a closer look at Psalm 83.

While many have promoted the idea of a Psalm 83 war in the near future, the main proponent of this view is Bill Salus, who is a friend of mine and a good man whom I respect. He has written a book titled *Isralestine*, which sets forth his thesis. Salus says, "Soon to come is a major and devastating war in the Middle East between the confederacy of Psalm 83:5-8 and the exceedingly great army of Israel. The previous Arab advances against Israel will be child's play compared to this final confederate attempt."[3] He views Psalm 83 as the missing key "that completes the final piece of the prophetic puzzle."[4]

This view of Psalm 83 is gaining ground among many prophecy teachers. I've read many articles about it in recent days and have heard many prophecy teachers refer to it in their sermons and messages. Those who hold to this view see the current uprisings in the Middle East as a major step or prophetic shift of gears toward the fulfillment of the alliance and war predicted in this psalm.

Before we go on to examine this view in more detail, we first need to understand the context of Psalm 83.

The Context of Psalm 83

Psalm 83 was written about 3000 years ago by Asaph, a singer appointed by David. It is a community or corporate lament that describes a crisis faced by the nation of Israel and appeals to the Lord for deliverance:

> O God, do not remain quiet; do not be silent and, O God, do not be still. For behold, Your enemies make an uproar, and those who hate You have exalted themselves. They make shrewd plans against Your people, and conspire together against Your treasured ones. They have said, "Come, and let us wipe them out as a nation, that the name of Israel be remembered no more." For they have conspired together with one mind; against You they make a covenant: The tents of Edom and the Ishmaelites, Moab and the Hagrites; Gebal and Ammon and Amalek, Philistia with the inhabitants of Tyre; Assyria also has joined with them; they have become a help to the children of Lot. Deal with them as with Midian, as with Sisera and Jabin at the torrent of Kishon, who were destroyed at En-dor, who became as dung for the ground. Make their nobles like Oreb and Zeeb and all their princes like Zebah and Zalmunna, who said, "Let us possess for ourselves the pastures of God."
>
> O my God, make them like the whirling dust, like chaff before the wind. Like fire that burns the forest and like a flame that sets the mountains on fire, so pursue them with Your tempest and terrify them with Your storm. Fill their faces with dishonor, that they

may seek Your name, O LORD. Let them be ashamed and dismayed forever, and let them be humiliated and perish, that they may know that You alone, whose name is the LORD, are the Most High over all the earth.

The psalm lists ten specific ancient enemies of Israel, using names that were familiar to the people at the time it was written. Salus identifies the modern counterparts to the ancient peoples listed in Psalm 83:

> Edom (Palestinian Refugees and Southern Jordanians)
>
> Ishmaelites (Saudi Arabians)
>
> Moab (Palestinian Refugees and Central Jordanians)
>
> Hagrites (Egyptians) [I disagree with this one][5]
>
> Gebal (Northern Lebanese)
>
> Ammon (Palestinian Refugees and Northern Jordanians)
>
> Amalek (Arabs south of Israel)
>
> Philistia (Palestinian Refugees and Hamas of the Gaza Strip)
>
> Tyre (Hezbollah and Southern Lebanese)
>
> Assyria (Syria and perhaps Northern Iraq)

Some argue that Psalm 83 was fulfilled in the days of Jehoshaphat, the king of Judah. We read in 2 Chronicles 20 that Jehoshaphat was threatened by a coalition comprised of Edom, Moab, and Ammon, and God saved Judah by causing the three nations to fight among themselves. Others believe Psalm 83 was fulfilled more recently during the Six-Day War in June 1967. However, neither of these events fit the precise specifications given in Psalm 83, so we must search for another solution. I will present the three main options that prophecy teachers hold to, then will explain why I believe the third one makes the most sense.

The Possible Explanations

Option #1: Psalm 83 Paves the Way for Ezekiel 38–39

It is alleged by Bill Salus and many others today that the Psalm 83 war, which involves the "near enemies" or "inner circle" of Israel's enemies, will serve as a precursor and catalyst for the Ezekiel 38 war, which concerns Israel's "far enemies" or "outer circle" of hostile nations. They believe this war will occur very soon, certainly before the Tribulation period, and possibly even before the rapture. Salus maintains that this Psalm 83 war *must* occur before the Tribulation and will clear out Israel's nearest surrounding enemies, paving the way for Israel to enjoy peace, security, and prosperity as well as greatly expand its borders, thus setting the stage for the attack described in Ezekiel 38. He says,

> Because of the judgments made upon the Arabs who despise them, Israel will attain the autonomy required to set the stage for the Russian-Iranian-led attack. The world will internationally esteem Israel as the sovereign Jewish State, and the Arab-Israeli conflict we witness today will be finally resolved. As such, Israel will be a nation of peace achieved via their military might.[6]

One key issue with this interpretation is that Psalm 83 doesn't say when it will be fulfilled. Salus surmises that the Psalm 83 war must occur before the war of Ezekiel 38–39 because that passage says Israel will be at peace when the Ezekiel 38–39 war breaks out. When making his case, he uses phrases like *we can safely presume* and *we deduce* in his attempt to conclude that the fulfillment of Psalm 83 must precede the Tribulation. It's fine to speculate and try to put the prophetic pieces of the puzzle together, but when we do so and try to arrive at firm conclusions, we run into problems.

For example, Salus notes, "We deduce this by recollecting that the Russian-Iranian coalition will attempt to invade a militarily secure Israel. This condition of security becomes a reality only subsequent to the judgments executed upon the surrounding Psalm 83 nations."[7] Yet this is all deduction and presumption without any solid basis in the text. Psalm 83 never gives any general or specific chronological indicators of when the events it describes will occur.

Ezekiel 38, on the other hand, tells us specifically that the invasion by Gog and Magog will occur in "the latter years" (Ezekiel 38:8) and "the last days" (Ezekiel 38:16), when Israel is regathered to her land and living at rest and securely. This pinpoints the time of the war to only a few, limited options in the end times. Psalm 83 provides no such chronological indicators. The future options for its fulfillment are wide open. It *may* precede the invasion of Ezekiel 38, but then again, it *may not*. There's no way to be certain or dogmatic about this.

Salus and others have constructed a scenario based on deductions that have no firm foundation in the text of Psalm 83 itself. They conclude that since the nations in Psalm 83 are not specifically mentioned in Ezekiel 38, they must be destroyed earlier to pave the way for the climate of rest and security Israel will enjoy. This is possible, but God could achieve His purposes in other ways. For example, the covenant the Antichrist signs with Israel in Daniel 9:27 could be the source of the peace Israel enjoys at the time of the Ezekiel 38 invasion.

Option #2: Psalm 83 Is Connected to Ezekiel 38–39

A second way to look at Psalm 83 is to see it in connection with Ezekiel 38–39. Salus maintains that Psalm 83 must precede Ezekiel 38, but it's also possible that it could be part of it. Here are a few of the similarities between these two texts:

	PSALM 83	**EZEKIEL 38–39**
The Plan	"They make shrewd plans against your people, and conspire together"	"It will come about on that day, that thoughts will come into your mind and you will devise an evil plan" (38:10)
The Purpose	"Come, and let us wipe them out as a nation, that the name of Israel be remembered no more" (v. 4)	"You will go up, you will come like a storm; you will be like a cloud covering the land" (38:9)
The Judgment	"Deal with them as with Midian" (reference to	"Every man's sword will be against his brother" (infighting) (38:21)

	Judges 7 when the Midianites killed each other) (v. 9)	
	"Like fire that burns the forest and a flame that sets the mountain on fire" (v. 14)	"a torrential rain, with hailstones, fire and brimstone" (38:22)
The Result	"That they may know that You alone, whose name is the LORD, are the Most High over all the earth" (v. 18)	"And the nations will know that I am the LORD, the Holy One in Israel" (39:7)

Another interesting similarity is that each passage mentions ten proper names in connection with an invading coalition.

The most obvious difference between these two passages is the nations listed as part of the coalition against Israel. In Ezekiel 38:1-6, the far enemies of Israel are set forth as far as one could go in every direction—Russia (Rosh) to the far north, Iran (Persia) to the east, Sudan (Cush) to the south, and Libya (Put) to the west. However, in Psalm 83, the near enemies of Israel are listed: Lebanon, Jordan, Gaza, and others, depending upon the precise identifications. If these two passages are complementary—that is, if they are describing the same invasion— how are we to account for these differences? It is possible that while Ezekiel 38 lists the far nations in every direction from Israel, the near enemies are also included, even though they are not specifically named. The reason that's possible is Ezekiel

38:6 ends with these words: "many peoples with you." That could be a catch all to indicate that not every nation that will participate in the invasion is named. If this is true, that would leave room for unlisted nations to have part in the invasion.

Another difference between the two passages is the purpose for the invasions. As pointed out in the recent chart, in both passages, the coalitions come to wipe out or cover the land. But Ezekiel 38:12 adds the extra detail that they will come "to capture spoil and to seize plunder." However, that doesn't make these purposes contradictory or mutually exclusive. I would submit that the coalitions come to wipe out the Jews *and* plunder their land. Both are true. The people of Israel will be conquered and plundered.

One other alleged problem with viewing Psalm 83 and Ezekiel 38 as the same event is that in Psalm 83 some would argue that Saudi Arabia (the Ishmaelites) is part of the coalition, whereas in Ezekiel 38:13 Sheba and Dedan are sitting on the sidelines protesting the invasion. Of course, this assumes that the Ishmaelites and Sheba and Dedan refer to the same geographical location. The Ishmaelites is probably a general term for "all the Bedouin tribe who dwelt in tents and invaded Judah from the south or for the seminomads who made their living from the caravan trades."[8] Sheba and Dedan refer more specifically to the area we know today as Saudi Arabia and the Gulf States. If these identifications are correct, then there is no problem with viewing Psalm 83 and Ezekiel 38–39 as parallel passages.

Option #3: Psalm 83 Is a Prototype

While option two is possible, there is a third way to interpret

Psalm 83 that I believe is best. It basically involves understanding it as being similar to Psalm 2, which says,

> Why are the nations in an uproar and the peoples devising a vain thing? The kings of the earth take their stand and the rulers take counsel together against the LORD and against His Anointed, saying, "Let us tear their fetters apart and cast away their cords from us!"
>
> He who sits in the heavens laughs, the Lord scoffs at them. Then He will speak to them in His anger and terrify them in His fury, saying, "But as for Me, I have installed My King upon Zion, My holy mountain.
>
> "I will surely tell of the decree of the LORD: He said to Me, 'You are My Son, today I have begotten You. Ask of Me, and I will surely give the nations as Your inheritance, and the very ends of the earth as Your possession. You shall break them with a rod of iron, You shall shatter them like earthenware.'"
>
> Now therefore, O kings, show discernment; take warning, O judges of the earth. Worship the LORD with reverence and rejoice with trembling. Do homage to the Son, that He not become angry, and you perish in the way, for His wrath may soon be kindled. How blessed are all who take refuge in Him!

Psalm 2 highlights the ages-long hatred and conspiracy of the nations against the Lord and His anointed One, the Messiah. The similarities with Psalm 83 are apparent. Nations are plotting and conspiring against the Lord and the Davidic King. The Lord scoffs at them and predicts a time when they will be

destroyed and His King will rule the earth and people will submit to Him. This looks ahead to the messianic kingdom or the
1000-year reign of Christ that culminates the end times. The
main difference between these two passages is that in Psalm 2
the nations are not specifically enumerated, whereas ten specific enemies are listed in Psalm 83. But the point is the same:
The enemies of God and His anointed King will one day be
destroyed and will submit to Him. People don't look for a separate Psalm 2 war, but see it as a general prophecy that the Lord's
enemies will be destroyed in the end times. I believe that's the
same thing we see going on in Psalm 83.

We have to remember that the Psalms were written long
before the prophets began to write and give specific prophecies concerning the nations. The prophets are where we look to
find detailed information concerning the various world powers and end-time events. There are certainly messianic prophecies in the Psalms, but I'm not aware of other specific, detailed
prophecies in the Psalms concerning the Gentile nations in the
end times except for a few places that mention them turning to
the true God (Psalm 45:12; 68:31; 87:4) or a general statement
of future judgment (Psalm 137:7-9). I believe that constructing
a separate end-time war out of Psalm 83 is reading too much
into a text that is simply saying that Israel has been and always
will be surrounded by enemies and that someday the Lord will
finally deal with them. It could be that this national lament
during the Davidic reign is raising the ubiquitous questions
for Israel: Why does everyone hate us? When will it ever end?
Will God ever destroy the enemies who hound us? The people
cry out to the Lord in prayer and trust that He will hear their

cry and destroy their enemies. In Psalm 83, God encouraged the nation and its king at the very beginning of the Davidic reign by telling them He will ultimately prevail over His enemies and will protect His people from extinction.

Commenting on Psalm 83, Warren Wiersbe said, "Israel has been the object of hatred and opposition since their years in Egypt, but God has kept His promise and preserved them (Gen. 12:1-3). Pharaoh, Haman (the book of Esther), Hitler, and every other would-be destroyer of the Jews has ultimately been humiliated and defeated."[9] In other words, Israel will always be surrounded by enemies seeking her destruction, but God will destroy them all. Psalm 83 offers assurance to the newly established Davidic dynasty that God will ultimately destroy Israel's enemies.

Old Testament scholar Derek Kidner wrote, "It may well be, then, that this is a prayer concerned with something bigger than a single threat and a particular alliance: rather with the perennial aggression of the world against God and His people. The psalm may have been the product of a habitual consciousness of this."[10]

Following this same line of thinking, James Montgomery Boice said,

> We know of no time in Israel's history when these ten powers were actually arrayed against her, so the listing in verses 6-8 is probably a generalization. It is a way of saying that the Jews always seem to be surrounded by enemies and in danger of being liquidated. This has been the actual condition of Israel throughout history as many peoples and nations have arrayed themselves against her.[11]

I would add to Boice's statement that Psalm 83 will be fulfilled in the future at some time—perhaps when all the nations are judged at the final great war of Armageddon. There doesn't have to be a Psalm 83 war for the psalm to be literally fulfilled. Rather, the text lists for us Israel's inveterate enemies, the nations that constantly seduced and oppressed Israel throughout her history, and acknowledges that God will ultimately bring judgment against those enemies. That is the view I prefer with regard to Psalm 83.

Concluding Thoughts on Psalm 83

While I like Bill Salus and appreciate the diligent work he has done in setting forth the thesis for a separate Psalm 83 war, I don't see a separate Psalm 83 war taking place before the Tribulation occurs. While there will be wars and rumors of wars and nation rising against nation in the end times, I believe Scripture points to two major wars involving Israel during the last days—the Gog and Magog war during the first half of the Tribulation and the battle of Armageddon at the culmination of the Tribulation. The prophets never clearly delineate a war like the one Salus proposes from Psalm 83. If this war plays the central role that Salus alleges it does, one would expect the prophets to have addressed this directly. But that didn't happen.

The time of security and rest Israel enjoys immediately prior to the Ezekiel 38 invasion doesn't have to result from the annihilation of Israel's near enemies. Rather, the presence of that peace could be just as easily explained as being a result of the peace treaty that the Antichrist brokers with Israel. Of course, God could wipe out some of the near enemies of Israel in the near future, or Israel could end up in a war against some of them and gain the upper hand.

While we don't have every piece of the prophectic puzzle provided for us in Scripture, we can know these facts with certainty: Israel will always find herself surrounded by enemies. She will know constant persecution and even the threat of extinction. And she will know God's supernatural deliverance at the battle of Gog and Magog and then again in the battle of Armageddon, when Christ returns from heaven to deal with His enemies once and for all.

Chapter 9

Will Syria Be Destroyed Soon?

There can be no peace without Syria.[1]

HENRY KISSINGER

D uring the spring of 2011, the flames of revolt sweeping the Middle East blew into a nation many thought would be immune to such unrest—Syria. So many were surprised when Syria became caught up in the Arab inferno, with protesters voicing their objections to the regime of Bashar al-Assad.

The Assad family has ruled Syria with an iron fist for 41 years. The family comes from "the Alawite mountains overlooking the Mediterranean which is a stronghold of the secretive sect with links to Shi'ite Islam."[2] This Alawite minority rules the Sunni majority in Syria; thus, the ingredients are present for long-standing grudges and the desire for payback. The Shiite background of the Assad family has made them a natural ally of Iran and Iran's Lebanese proxy, Hezbollah, who are also Shiites. Syria has been a willing partner in the Shiite crescent that Iran aspires to create to extend its dominant position over the Middle East. In 2005 Syria signed a mutual defense pact with Iran, in which Syria agreed to allow the deployment of Iranian weapons on its territory. Syria and Iran signed an additional defense agreement in December 2009 with "common enemies and challenges"[3] in mind.

When the unrest erupted in Syria, Assad quickly blamed "conspirators" for the protests. Many are wondering if the Assad regime will ultimately fall in the same way Mubarak was ousted in Egypt. However, according to Reuters, "Senior Syrian army ranks are packed with loyal members of President Bashar al-Assad's Alawite minority, reducing any prospect of military pressure on him to stand aside if protests grow."[4] As long as the military stands with Assad, he and his cruel regime will likely remain safe. Assad and his acolytes have shown themselves willing to use brutal means and bloody crackdowns to quell any meaningful dissent, but in the current environment, that may not be enough if the masses turn to the streets in full and sustained revolt. Only time will tell how all this will play out in Syria.

One ally that has come to Syria's defense and offered unwavering support for the bloody crackdowns is the Lebanese terrorist group and Iranian surrogate Hezbollah. This terrorist organization has a great deal to lose if Bashar Assad is deposed. Besides receiving cash from Syria, Hezbollah is also believed to receive Iranian weapons shipments through the country. In a 2011 speech on "Liberation Day" which marks the withdrawal of the Israeli army from southern Lebanon in 2000, Sheik Hassan Nasrallah, the leader of Hezbollah, said, "Overthrowing the regime in Syria is in the American and Israeli interest. They want to overthrow the regime and replace it with a moderate regime."[5] It serves Hezbollah's purposes to have a radical ally in Syria.

The unrest in Syria, added to all the other upheaval in

the Middle East, has left Israel on edge. Syria has been an entrenched enemy of Israel since the formation of the modern state. The two nations have fought against each other in three bloody wars: the War of Independence (1948), the Six-Day War (1967), and the Yom Kippur War (1973). Syria has been greatly emboldened by the Hezbollah War waged against Israel for 34 days in the summer of 2006. The nation has assumed a much more aggressive stance and intensified the bellicose rhetoric against Israel in recent years.

In September 2007, Israel destroyed Syria's Deiz ez Zor nuclear plant in northern Syria, which heightened the already tense standoff between the nations. A confidential report in 2011 by the International Atomic Energy Agency (IAEA), the UN nuclear watchdog, says the Deir ez Zor site was a covert nuclear plant designed to produce plutonium. The IAEA officially stated "that Syria was constructing a covert nuclear reactor, and we believe that reactor was designed to produce plutonium for possible use in nuclear weapons."[6] To complicate matters, Russia has stepped up and is considering helping Syria build a nuclear reactor.

The new nuclear angle, along with the recent upheaval in Syria, has added to Israel's angst. The fear of the unknown can be worse than the known, even if it's unsavory. Syria is a formidable military foe. It has spent $3 billion in the last three years on weapons, up from less than $100 million in 2002. Syria now has more troops and tanks, and nearly as many aircraft as Israel.

> Syria has reportedly received $1 billion from Iran in 2007-8 to buy surface-to-surface missiles, rockets,

anti-tank missiles and anti-aircraft systems. According to *Haaretz* (March 21, 2008), "Israel has learned that Syria is buying more missiles than tanks, on the assumption that attacking the Israeli home front would deter Israel on the one hand, and help to determine the war on the other." A Syrian delegation visiting Moscow in May 2008 was reportedly seeking a variety of new weapons systems that Israel views as threatening. Israel is particularly concerned with a Syrian request for long-range S-300 surface-to-air missiles that could threaten IAF jets flying on the Israeli side of the Golan Heights. Syria also reportedly wants MiG 29 fighter jets and the Iskander surface-to-surface missile system, which is a longer range and more accurate missile than the ballistic missiles currently in Syria's arsenal. The Syrian navy, which currently has no submarines, is apparently also looking to purchase two Amur-1650 submarines from Russia.[7]

While considered inferior to Israel's military might, "the Assad regime fields armed forces totaling more than 380,000 men, with another 130,000 troops in reserve. Syria's arsenal includes approximately 3,700 tanks and some 510 combat aircraft."[8] If this military machine were to fall into even more radical hands, all bets would be off for Israel. *The Los Angeles Times* reported this about growing Israeli fears concerning the unrest in Syria:

> As popular unrest threatens to topple another Arab neighbor, Israel finds itself again quietly rooting for the survival of an autocratic yet predictable regime,

rather than face an untested new government in its place. Syrian President Bashar Assad's race to tamp down public unrest is stirring anxiety in Israel that is even higher than its hand-wringing over Egypt's recent regime change. Unlike Israel and Egypt, Israel and Syria have no peace agreement, and Syria, with a large arsenal of sophisticated weapons, is one of Israel's strongest enemies…Israel is worried about what might happen to Syria's arsenal, including Scud missiles, thousands of rockets capable of reaching all of Israel, chemical warheads, advanced surface-to-air systems and an aging air force. "You want to work with the devil you know," said Moshe Maoz, a former government advisor and Syria expert at Hebrew University's Harry S. Truman Institute for the Advancement of Peace.[9]

Israel now has one more concern to add to its growing list of worries about its future and the future of the region. If Assad were to fall, whoever succeeds him would almost certainly be more radical and could push the already-dire situation over the brink, triggering an all-out conflagration. Or the nation could fracture into tribal sects rife with instability. Or, in an attempt to galvanize the nation and arouse nationalistic fervor, Assad could instigate some sort of showdown with Israel. Any of these scenarios are possible, and any of them could bring Israel to feel compelled to act preemptively against Syria. Could it be that another nightmarish military conflict is just around the corner? Many believe this is where we're headed, and many believe this is exactly what the Bible predicts for Syria in the near future. This view is based on an ancient prophecy found in Isaiah 17.

Syria in Bible Prophecy

One of the next key end-time events, according to many prophecy teachers, is the destruction of Damascus, the capital of Syria. We read about this event in Isaiah 17:1-2, which says, "The oracle concerning Damascus. 'Behold, Damascus is about to be removed from being a city and will become a fallen ruin. The cities of Aroer are forsaken; they will be for flocks to lie down in, and there will be no one to frighten them.'"

Those who say the passage points to a future destruction maintain that Damascus has never "become a fallen ruin," so if this prophecy is to be literally fulfilled, it must occur in the future. Specifics about how this will occur differ, but many believe this prophecy predicts an Israeli nuclear attack on Damascus.

It's also often alleged that the supernatural destruction of Syria will occur either before or right after the rapture of the church. Some believe this could happen at any time in the near future. Here's a representative statement in support of this view:

> In the last days, the Bible tells us of a horrible series of events that will take place in the lands of Israel and Syria. One of these events is the disappearance of Damascus as one of the premiere cities in the world... In the very near future, Damascus will once again play a major role in human events. The prophet Isaiah provides us with God's commentary on a future conflict

between Damascus and Israel, and in so doing, he reveals certain prophecies which have been partially fulfilled in the past. However, the ultimate fulfillment of Isaiah 17 remains in the future. The current existence of Damascus, which will one day cease to be a city, as well as the historical absence of the coalition of nations prophesied to attack Israel and be destroyed by God, is proof that Isaiah 17 prophesies events yet future.[10]

When the Isaiah 17 text is quoted, often only the first two verses are cited. But if we keep reading past those verses, it becomes apparent that at the time the demise of Damascus occurs, Israel will also suffer devastation. In Isaiah's day, Ephraim was the name for the northern kingdom of Israel. With that in mind, read Isaiah 17:3-7, and notice that at the same time Damascus is destroyed, Israel is too:

> "The fortified city will disappear from Ephraim [the 10 northern tribes of Israel], and sovereignty from Damascus and the remnant of Aram; they will be like the glory of the sons of Israel," declares the LORD of hosts. Now in that day the glory of Jacob will fade, and the fatness of his flesh will become lean. It will be even like the reaper gathering the standing grain, as his arm harvests the ears, or it will be like one gleaning ears of grain in the valley of Rephaim. Yet gleanings will be left in it like the shaking of an olive tree, two or three olives on the topmost bough, four or five on the branches of a fruitful tree, declares the LORD, the God of Israel. In that day man will have regard for

his Maker and his eyes will look to the Holy One of
Israel (Isaiah 17:3-7).

When we read Isaiah 17:1-2 and 17:3-7 together, we are
forced to conclude that at the same time Damascus suffers devastation, Israel will also fall. Some try to argue that the mention
of Ephraim refers to Palestinian territory that will also suffer
defeat at the same time as Damascus, but that seems a rather
far-fetched argument. I've heard others say that the nuclear
fallout from Israel's strike on Damascus will be the culprit that
cripples Israel, but this seems to be a stretch as well.

I believe it makes more sense to hold that Isaiah 17 was
fulfilled in the eighth century BC when both Damascus, the
capital of Syria, and Samaria, the capital of Israel, were ham-
mered by the Assyrians. In that conquest, both Damascus and
Samaria were destroyed, just as Isaiah 17 predicts. According
to history, Tiglath-pileser III (745-727 BC) pushed vigorously
to the west, and in 734 the Assyrians advanced and laid siege
to Damascus, which fell two years later in 732. Rezin, the Syrian monarch, was executed, his kingdom was overthrown, and
the city suffered the fate that a few years later befell Samaria.

The view that Isaiah 17 was fulfilled in the eighth century
BC is further supported by the final three verses of Isaiah 17:

> Alas, the uproar of many peoples who roar like the
> roaring of the seas, and the rumbling of nations who
> rush on like the rumbling of mighty waters! The
> nations rumble on like the rumbling of many waters,
> but He will rebuke them and they will flee far away,
> and be chased like chaff in the mountains before the

wind, or like whirling dust before a gale. At evening time, behold, there is terror! Before morning they are no more. Such will be the portion of those who plunder us and the lot of those who pillage us (verses 12-14).

Some try to see this passage as a future reference to Israel gaining supremacy over its enemies in the end times, but this is a historical reference to God's destruction of the Assyrian army under Sennacherib in 701 BC, when Sennacherib led a military campaign against Judah and Hezekiah the king. The Assyrians get their just desserts when they are destroyed by God. Isaiah 17:14 vividly points this out: "At evening time, behold, there is terror! Before morning they are no more." Isaiah 37:36-38 records the fulfillment of this, when 185,000 Assyrians fell in one night under the hand of divine judgment.

In Jeremiah 49:23-27 we find another biblical prophecy that describes the destruction of Damascus. This passage refers to what occurred in 605 BC when Nebuchadnezzar, king of Babylon, swept through the ancient Near East wreaking havoc upon nation after nation. Nebuchadnezzar is mentioned several times in this section of Jeremiah, which serves to confirm that this prophecy was fulfilled in this time period (46:2,13; 49:28).

Still, there are some who contend Isaiah 17:1 has not yet been fulfilled. They ask, "When was this ever literally fulfilled in the past?" Let's look again at what the verse says: "Behold, Damascus is about to be removed from being a city and will become a fallen ruin." The King James Version says here, "Behold, Damascus is taken away from being a city, and it shall be a ruinous heap." The ESV reads, "Behold, Damascus will cease to be a city and will become a heap of ruins." The NIV says, "See, Damascus will no longer be a city but will become a heap of ruins."

To determine whether Isaiah 17:1 has been fulfilled or not, we have to carefully note what the text *does* and *does not* say. It *does* say Damascus will be destroyed and made a heap of ruins and will be "removed from being a city." That literally occurred in 732 BC when Damascus was destroyed by the Assyrians under Tiglath-pileser. Note also that the text *does not* say Damascus would be removed *forever* from being a city. It simply says that Damascus will be "removed" or "taken away" from being a city. Isaiah 17 is a prophecy of a temporary desolation that happened to many nations in the ancient Near East when they were destroyed by invading armies. Nowhere does Isaiah say that Damascus would never be rebuilt or inhabited again. Thus we can conclude that Isaiah 17 was indeed fulfilled in the ancient past.

What Is Syria's Future?

Having said that, I do believe that events today in Syria point toward the fulfillment of biblical prophecies that have not yet come to pass. As the fuse on the Middle East powder keg continues to burn, the stage is being set for the Middle East peace treaty prophesied in Daniel 9:27. The only solution to the Middle East quagmire, short of all-out conflagration, is some kind of comprehensive peace agreement for the whole region. In the current Middle East environment, with Syria as a key player and its growing military prowess, it makes sense that it would be necessary for Syria to have a part in any such peace agreement. After all, as Henry Kissinger observed, "There can be no peace in the Middle East without Syria."[11]

As we saw in Ezekiel 38–39 and even Psalm 83, the futures of many nations are predicted in Scripture. But there are still pieces of the prophetic puzzle that we don't have, so we cannot ascertain every aspect of what is yet to come. That happens to be the case with Syria. Because Isaiah 17 and Jeremiah's prophecies about Syria were fulfilled in the past, we cannot turn to them for insight about what will happen to Syria during the end times. Even so, we can rest assured that Syria will eventually experience a day of judgment, just like all the other nations who come against Israel and the Lord.

Chapter 10

Where's America?

America is not mentioned anywhere in the Bible, implying that it would be crippled or taken out of the picture in some way.

GLENN BECK (APRIL 2009)

T he Middle East is on fire, and everyone is wondering where it's all headed. At the same time, however, large numbers of people are asking, "But what about America? What role will it play during the end times?"

While America is still the lone superpower in the world, in recent years, American influence in the Middle East has been waning. More alarming is the fact American support for Israel has been slipping rapidly. If America ceases to have its current level of superpower influence, how will that affect world events? What does the Bible say, if anything, about America's future?

I've been asked these questions so many times that I wrote a book to address them. It's titled *The Late Great United States: What Bible Prophecy Reveals about America's Last Days.* The thesis of the book is that America is not mentioned in the Bible, either directly or indirectly, and that this silence is significant.

America is not Babylon the Great in Revelation 17–18, the unnamed nation in Isaiah 18, the ten lost tribes of Israel, or the "young lions of Tarshish" in Ezekiel 38:13. In fact, America is missing in action when it comes to the end-time prophecies of the Bible.

The Scriptures reveal that the major superpower in the end times, at least by the midpoint of the Tribulation, will be a reunited Roman Empire (Revelation 13:4). This European dominance over world affairs can only be explained in light of America's decline. The late prophecy scholar John Walvoord saw no major end-time role for America. He wrote, "Although conclusions concerning the role of America in prophecy in the end time are necessarily tentative, the Scriptural evidence is sufficient to conclude that America in that day will not be a major power and apparently does not figure largely in either the political, economic, or religious aspects of the world."[1] Charles Ryrie agrees:

> The Bible has made crystal clear the destiny of many nations. Babylon, Persia, Greece, Rome, Egypt, Russia, and Israel…But not so with the United States… The Bible's silence concerning the future of the United States might well mean that she will play no prominent role in the end-time drama. A nation does not have to be named in order to be identified in Bible prophecy. When Ezekiel described the future Russian invasion he used the phrase "remote parts of the north" (38:15). Surely some prophet would have predicted something about those countries or peoples in the remote parts of the West if God had intended a major

end-time role for them in the Western Hemisphere. The fact is that no one did…Instead, we are led to conclude that the United States will be neutralized, subordinated, or wiped out, thus having little or no part in the political and military affairs of the end time.[2]

To be sure, I don't want to see the United States decline. I love this country and all that has made it so special, but after much careful examination of the Scriptures, it does seem unlikely that the United States will play a key role in the end times. Which raises the following questions: What might happen that would reduce America to a subordinate role? What kind of event could bring America to its knees? While we cannot speak with certainty at this point—because the Bible doesn't tell us anything—we can make some educated guesses. Several plausible scenarios fit what we see taking place around us today. They could occur one by one over a period of time, or merge together to hasten a downward spiral.

The Threats to America

Over the last few years, we have witnessed major developments on three fronts that threaten the continued role of America as the world's superpower. These three fronts are moral (internal decay), military (external threat of nuclear terror), and monetary (economic hazard of a diminishing role for America and the dollar) in nature. Let's briefly consider each of these mounting perils.

Moral Malaise

For America, the news on the moral front is not good. We

are rapidly approaching a disastrous 50 percent out-of-wedlock birthrate. The dreaded scourge of abortion continues unabated with the total now over 50 million babies aborted since 1973. Pornography, a $12 billion-plus industry, is infecting our young people every day. According to the Center for Disease Control, 26 percent of American girls between the ages of 14-19 have at least one sexually transmitted disease.[3] And homosexual activists continue to propel their agenda forward, pushing America more and more toward the pouring out of judgment described in Romans 1:26-32. This passage tells how God will unleash His wrath against people by abandoning them to the ravaging consequences of their sin.

> For this reason God gave them over to dishonorable passions. For their women exchanged the natural sexual relations for unnatural ones, and likewise the men also abandoned natural relations with women and were inflamed in their passions for one another. Men committed shameless acts with men and received in themselves the due penalty for their error. And just as they did not see fit to acknowledge God, God gave them over to a depraved mind, to do what should not be done. They are filled with every kind of unrighteousness, wickedness, covetousness, malice. They are rife with envy, murder, strife, deceit, hostility. They are gossips, slanderers, haters of God, insolent, arrogant, boastful, contrivers of all sorts of evil, disobedient to parents, senseless, covenant-breakers, heartless, ruthless. Although they fully know God's righteous decree that those who practice such things deserve to

die, they not only do them but also approve of those who practice them (NET).

As you read those verses, did you catch the repetition of the phrase "God gave them over" (verses 24,26,28)? This tells us God judges people by abandoning them to their sin. Here in America, during the 1960s we experienced what is often called the sexual revolution, and that has been followed by the homosexual revolution. This has placed America on a downward trajectory, and at the time of this writing, homosexual marriage is now allowed in Iowa, Massachusetts, Vermont, New Hampshire, New York, Connecticut, and the District of Columbia. Several other states permit civil unions or domestic partnerships, and the number of states that will allow such is growing. An ABC-*Washington Post* survey in March 2011 found that 53 percent of Americans now support gay marriage. An Associated Press poll in August 2010 found 52 percent of Americans think the federal government should extend legal recognition to married gay couples, up from 46 percent the year before.[4] Indeed, the sexual revolution of Romans 1:24-25 has been followed by the homosexual revolution of Romans 1:26-27.

Interestingly, while approval of gay marriage is on the rise, Americans also have a growing sense that things are not right—that the nation is coming off the rails morally. In a recent Gallup Poll (May 2011), Americans were asked about their perception of moral values in the country. When asked, "How would you rate the overall state of moral values in this country—as excellent, good, only fair, or poor?" 45 percent of respondents answered poor, and only 15 percent said excellent or good.

In response to the question, "Right now, do you think the state of moral values in the country as a whole is getting better or worse?" 76 percent said it's getting worse, and only 14 percent said it's getting better. Here's a summary of what people said regarding the causes of the decline:

> Most commonly, respondents see a lack of respect for other people and a more general decline in moral values and standards. But the responses are quite varied. Specifically, some blame the perceived decline on poor parenting—specifically, parents not instilling proper values in their children. Some cite the poor examples of U.S. leaders in government and business who find themselves embroiled in ethical or moral scandals. And some reference larger societal factors, such as rising crime and violence, Americans turning away from God, church and religion, and the breakdown of the typical two-parent family.[5]

It is clear that America is hemorrhaging from within. Thomas Macauley, a British Parliamentarian, wrote these sobering words about the United States in 1857: "Your Republic will be as fearfully plundered and laid waste by barbarians in the 20th century as the Roman Empire was in the 5th century, with this difference—the Huns and Vandals who ravaged the Roman Empire came from without, and your Huns and Vandals will have been engendered within your own country."[6] It now appears that the huns and vandals of moral rot are upon us. Romans 1 says that when open sexual sin is condoned, judgment has already begun. When people ask, "When is God going to judge America?" the answer is clear: He already is judging the nation by abandoning her, by giving her over to her own wicked desires. How much longer until America collapses? No one knows. But we who are Christians need to be praying for our nation and doing all we can to live godly lives and promote righteousness.

Military Attack

Due to its geographic position and military might, America has enjoyed a level of peace and security most other nations envy. The US has very rarely faced major attacks on its own soil, with the Japanese bombing of Pearl Harbor on December 7, 1941 and the terrorist attacks on September 11, 2001 being rare exceptions. While any future terrorist attacks on American soil would definitely be tragic, the most serious external threat America faces these days is the nightmare of nuclear terror—a nuclear 9/11. The possibility that this might ever happen may seem far-fetched to many, but there are people in the world who would like very much to bring havoc and ultimately nuclear devastation to America. Experts warn that the threat is growing and may be more likely than not in the next decade.

Pakistan is growing more unstable all the time and has an impressive nuclear arsenal that is expected to reach 200 nukes by 2021. North Korea is another potential source of nuclear hostility. Iran is trying to reach the nuclear finish line and develop a deliverable nuclear weapon. While no one wants to even think about it, America would be a prime target, along with Israel, for any nuclear terrorist efforts. Our nation's leaders know this and are doing all they can to stem the tide, but intelligence and military might can only do so much. It's only a matter of time before terrorists are able to get their hands on nuclear material and can detonate either a dirty bomb that spreads harmful radiation in a city, or an actual nuclear device. Of course, either of these scenarios would cause untold loss in human life and economic catastrophe, not to mention lingering psychological effects that would leave the nation in a state from which it is unable to recover.

Money Matters

The effects of the economic tsunami that hit the world in 2008 are still being felt today. Everyone knows that the American economy is still fragile and will fail if serious changes are not implemented soon. Unemployment still hovers above eight percent. Entitlement spending will doom America if it's not brought under control. It's no great surprise why America's stock is dropping in the world markets—America's national debt now stands at a staggering $14.4 trillion dollars…and counting. The numbers on America's infamous debt clock near New York's Times Square have been spinning faster and faster. More and more Americans are looking to the government for support, with cradle-to-grave entitlements leading us to have what is being dubbed "a nanny state." The words of Thomas Jefferson are a stark reminder and warning: "A government big enough to give you everything you want is strong enough to take everything you have."

Time magazine ran an article on April 6, 2009 titled "Is the Almighty Dollar Doomed?" The article chronicles the growing consensus that the days of the dollar reserve system are numbered. "It's the passing of an era," said Robert Hormats, vice chairman of Goldman Sachs International, who helped prepare summits for presidents Gerald R. Ford, Jimmy Carter, and Ronald Reagan. "The U.S. is becoming less dominant while other nations are gaining influence."[7]

According to the Office of Management and Budget, entitlement spending—which includes Medicare, Medicaid, Social Security, and other benefit programs—now accounts for 60 percent of all spending. According to *USA Today*, "The real drivers of looming deficits are Medicare, projected to grow from $516 billion this year to $932 billion in 2018, and Social Security, forecast to grow from $581 billion this year to $966 in 2018 as Baby Boomers retire."[8]

The United States could collapse under the weight of its own excess, greed, and big government.

Money and the Military

Debt is not just an economic issue. It affects other areas of life as well. For example, debt threatens the security and even the continued existence of nations. For instance, the US Air Force says it needs more money to maintain the US dominance of the skies that it's enjoyed for decades. The American military machine is aging due to the wars in Iraq and Afghanistan, and new fighters and technology are carrying bigger and bigger price tags. If the US economy hits hard enough times, hard decisions will have to be made and money allocations will have to be prioritized. That more funds are needed to support entitlement and other government programs will mean less funds for national defense, which would leave the United

States more vulnerable than ever. Past empires have fallen under the crushing weight of massive debt service and their resulting inability to fund their military. Hapsburg Spain, pre-revolutionary France, the Ottoman Empire, and even the British—in the build-up to World War II—all went the same way.[9]

Newsweek ran a cover article on December 7, 2009 with the title "How Great Empires Fall: Steep Debt, Slow Growth and High Spending Kill Empires—and America Could Be Next." The cover had a gripping picture of the US Capitol building upside down. Here are few key excerpts from the cover article, which was by Niall Ferguson:

> We won the Cold War and weathered 9/11 but now economic weakness is endangering our global power… if the United States succumbs to a fiscal crisis, as an increasing number of economic experts fear it may, then the entire balance of global economic power could shift…If the United States doesn't come up soon with a credible plan to restore the federal budget to balance over the next 5 to 10 years, the danger is very real that a debt crisis could lead to a major weakening of American power.[10]

Ferguson notes the critical nexus between a nation's debt explosion and the inevitable weakening of its military arsenal:

> This is how empires begin to decline. It begins with a debt explosion. It ends with an inexorable reduction in the Army, Navy, and Air Force…As interest payments eat into the budget, something has to give—and that something is nearly always defense

expenditure. On the Pentagon's present plan, defense spending is set to fall from above 4 percent now to 3.2 percent of GDP in 2015 and to 2.6 percent of GDP by 2028.[11]

This is known as the "arithmetic of imperial decline."[12] Without radical fiscal reform, America, unable to expend the necessary resources for its own defense, could become the next great superpower to fall irreparably on the imperial ash-heap of history.

America's financial woes could also eventually lead to a much more isolationist stance in the world. While in today's global society it's impossible not to interact economically and politically with other nations, Americans are weary of being the world's policeman. With two major wars grinding ever so slowly to a halt, and crushing debt problems, it is not difficult to envision America pulling back on the international front. If this happens, it could pave the way for Europe and other nations to assume greater leadership roles globally. That, in turn, could pave the way for Antichrist's arrival.

The Rapture and the End of America as We Know It

While the three scenarios we just discussed—moral decay, military threat, and monetary collapse—could each happen alone or strike in a crippling combination, there's one other event that could suddenly end life in America as we know it. That event is the rapture. Add in the rapture to all these problems spiraling out of control, and America will become a second-rate nation in the twinkling of an eye. The rapture will change everything! While there are believers in every nation worldwide, America has such a large number of believers percentage-wise that its population would be seriously decimated by the rapture. Think about the Dow Jones the next day. The unpaid mortgages. The loss of tax revenue. The cascade of bank failures. The greatly reduced workforce. And other serious repercussions.

The immediate removal of the spiritual salt and light from American society would certainly hasten God's judgment on America.

What Can We Do?

No one knows when the rapture will occur, or when America will fall. In the meantime, we must never forget to follow God's domestic policy for our nation by praying earnestly for our government leaders (1 Timothy 2:1-2), living righteous lives (Proverbs 14:34), sharing the good news with others (Romans 10:15), and blessing the Jewish people (Genesis 12:1-3). We must remember that the ultimate fate of a nation is not dependent upon politics, military might, or economics, but on righteousness, goodness, and mercy.

In recent years America has placed itself on slippery ground by undermining its support for Israel. While America is not obligated to agree with every policy decision Israel makes, the Scripture is clear that nations are cursed or blessed by God based on their treatment of the Jewish people. History has borne this out. I like to say that every time someone has tried to wipe out the Jewish people, the Jews end up with another holiday. With Pharaoh they got Passover, with Haman in the book of Esther they got Purim, with Antiochus Epiphanes they got Hanukkah, and with Hitler they got May 14, 1948, the rebirth of the modern nation of Israel.

God promised long ago that those who bless Abraham and his descendants will be blessed, and those who curse them will be cursed (Genesis 12:3). God has never abrogated this promise. Much of America's blessing as a nation can be traced to its benevolent treatment of the Jews and Israel.

But our nation's support—particularly from a political perspective—has waned dramatically under President Obama. In 2009 Obama publicly demanded that Israel halt all West Bank settlement activity as a condition for further talks with the Palestinians, a demand that even Palestinian negotiator Mahmoud Abbas has not made. Obama also announced demands on Israel during a visit to the UN, contributing to "the atmosphere of menace toward Israel" at the Israel-despising body.[13]

In May 2011, in his most egregious betrayal of Israel, President Obama called on the Jewish nation to return to the 1967 borders as the basis for the creation of a neighboring Palestinian State. This foolish demand has put the US squarely at odds with Israel. Israeli prime minister Netanyahu responded quickly and forthrightly:

> While Israel is prepared to make generous compromises for peace, it cannot go back to the 1967 lines. These lines are indefensible. Remember that, before 1967, Israel was all of nine miles wide. It was half the width of the Washington Beltway. And these were not the boundaries of peace; they were the boundaries of repeated wars, because the attack on Israel was so attractive.[14]

In the aftermath of Obama's remarks, I heard one Israeli official refer to the 1967 borders as "Auschwitz borders."

One of the surest ways for America to seal its doom is to turn its back on Israel and force the nation into a no-win situation. Again, while support of Israel doesn't mean it's necessary to agree with every policy decision the nation makes, stating that the Jewish people must return to the 1967 borders as a condition for so-called peace clearly puts America in an adversarial role.

As Mona Charen said about President Obama's posture toward Israel, "A false friend can do more damage than an open enemy."[15] America must remain a staunch supporter of Israel and a faithful ally. One of the secrets to America's greatness—in spite of all its other failures—has been its unwavering support of Israel, and God has blessed America per His promise in Genesis 12:3. However, if America continues on its current path and fails to bless the Jewish people, the final vestige of God's blessing upon our nation could be withdrawn, and the end could come quickly—very quickly.

Pray for our nation, and pray for our leaders!

Chapter 11

Scanning the Horizon

*We all live under the same sky,
but we don't all have the same horizon.*

Konrad Adenauer (German statesman)

Never before in human history has there been such a convergence of trends and developments that are part of the matrix of end-time events predicted in Scripture. And never before have world events had such an immediate, instantaneous impact on everyone. Events that decades ago would have taken months or even years to bring about change now take minutes. The widespread revolts in the Arab nations during the spring months of 2011 have changed the entire landscape of the Middle East in a matter of days and weeks. And in the ensuing months, that landscape will continue to morph before our eyes. The incredible acceleration of the pace at which all this is happening has contributed to a foreboding sense among many that we are moving rapidly toward a great crisis.

Up to this point, we have surveyed what the Bible predicts for the future of the Middle East and the world, and we have considered how current events might relate to what the Scriptures prophesy. From here onward, I want to try to tie our various threads of thought together and bring them into tighter focus.

Looking Ahead

In light of my study of Bible prophecy and what's taking place in the world today, what follows is an effort to try to put the pieces of the prophetic puzzle together. Below is a list of ten key events that I see looming on the horizon:

1. World tensions will continue to build. The nations will continue to turn against Israel as she struggles for survival in a sea of enemies. Israel, Islam, terror, the threat of nuclear jihad, Middle East revolutions, and oil crises will dominate world news, riveting everyone's attention on the Middle East and North Africa. The worldwide cry for peace, security, and stability will reach a deafening crescendo.

2. Someday, without any warning, Jesus will come to rapture His bride to heaven. All believers in Christ will be whisked away to the Father's house in heaven. All unbelievers will be left behind.

3. The United States will be greatly affected by the rapture, with millions of citizens suddenly gone. In the wake of the rapture's devastating effects on the US economy, there will be a dramatic shift of world power away from the US to Europe and Asia.

4. Out of the chaos and confusion created by the rapture, the Antichrist will rise from a reunited form of the Roman Empire led by an oligarchy or ruling

committee consisting of ten leaders. This revived or reunited Roman Empire will probably be some future form of the European Union. This final Roman prince will make a seven-year peace treaty with Israel, ushering in a brief season of worldwide peace (Daniel 9:27; Ezekiel 38:8,11; 1 Thessalonians 5:1-2; Revelation 6:1-2). The world will enter into a kind of new *Pax Romana* (Roman Peace).

5. In brokering the Middle East peace deal, Antichrist will temporarily end the threat of terror and instability and guarantee the uninterrupted flow of oil to the West. He will be hailed as a great peacemaker. At last, it will appear that the world has what it has waited for—peace and prosperity.

6. The world's utopia won't last long. Sometime during the first half of the Tribulation, the coalition of nations in Ezekiel 38 will stage a surprise attack on Israel, who has let down her guard. Russia's expanding power, influence, and alliances in the Middle East will be the hooks in the jaws that will drag her reluctantly into this course of action. The attack will be against both Israel and the West, since Israel will be joined to the Antichrist by her treaty. This could set the stage for the final great clash of civilizations.

7. God will supernaturally intervene, just like in Old Testament times, to rescue Israel from total annihilation and destroy the invaders.

8. The power vacuum created by the destruction of the armies of Russia, Iran, and Islamic coalition partners will be quickly filled by the Antichrist. He will seize this opportunity to invade Israel, breaking his covenant with the nation, and he will move against the helpless nations of Egypt, Libya, and Sudan as he launches his world empire at the midpoint of the seven-year Tribulation. He will establish a headquarters in Babylon (modern Iraq) and seize control of the great oil supply in the Persian Gulf.

9. The Great Tribulation—mentioned by Jesus in Matthew 24:21—will break out, plunging the world into its final days of darkness and dismay.

10. The world will be saved from the brink of destruction by the second coming of Jesus Christ. Christ will then establish His 1000-year kingdom of peace and righteousness on the earth.

In a book I helped update, titled *Armageddon, Oil and Terror*, we included the following "Prophetic Checklist for the Nations." I thought it might be helpful to repeat that checklist here.

A PROPHETIC CHECKLIST FOR THE NATIONS

The prophetic events regarding the nations and the last days can be compiled chronologically. Consider how the following list of significant events—past, present, and future—shows that the world is being dramatically prepared for end-time events.

1. The establishment of the United Nations began a serious first step toward world government.

2. The rebuilding of Europe after World War II made a revival of the Roman Empire possible.

3. Israel was re-established as a nation.

4. Russia rose to world power and became the ally of the Islamic world.

5. The Common Market and World Bank showed the need for some international regulation of the world economy.

6. China rose to world power and developed the capacity to field a massive army.

7. The Middle East became the most significant trouble spot in the world.

8. The oil blackmail awakened the world to the new concentration of wealth and power in the Middle East.

9. The Iron Curtain fell, removing the final barrier to the revival of the Roman Empire.

10. The world clamors for peace because of the continued disruption caused by the high price of oil, terrorist incidents, and the confused military situation in the Middle East.

11. Ten leaders (the "Group of Ten") will emerge from a European and Mediterranean coalition—beginnings of the last stage of the prophetic fourth world empire.

12. In a dramatic power play, a new Mediterranean leader will uproot three leaders of the coalition and take control of the powerful ten-leader group.

13. The new Mediterranean leader will negotiate a "final" peace settlement in the Middle East (broken three-and-a-half years later).

14. Russia and her Islamic allies will attempt an invasion of Israel, but will be miraculously destroyed.

15. The Mediterranean leader will proclaim himself world dictator, break his peace settlement with Israel, and declare himself to be God.

16. The new world dictator will desecrate the temple in Jerusalem.

17. The terrible judgments of the Great Tribulation will be poured out on the nations of the world.

18. Worldwide rebellion will threaten the world dictator's rule as armies from throughout the world converge on the Middle East for World War III.

19. Christ will return to earth with His armies from heaven.

20. The armies of the world will unite to resist Christ's coming and will be destroyed in the battle of Armageddon.

21. Christ will establish His millennial reign on earth, ending the times of the Gentiles.

You have to admit that is quite a forecast. The earth appears to be on the verge of entering into its most dangerous and

difficult days. In light of that, we all need to be praying con-
tinuously for the people who live in Middle Eastern and North
African nations. They are in the grip of false religion and brutal
dictators who oppress and take advantage of them. This is all
the more reason the church must seek to reach all of the Middle East and North Africa with the gospel of Jesus Christ before
it is too late. Please make a point of praying faithfully for the
dear people in these nations at this critical hour.

Another critical matter each of us should consider is where
we stand personally with the Lord. There's nothing we can do
that is more important. The Middle East is burning, times are
uncertain, and the prophetic signposts are lining up for the
last days, just the Bible predicted. Where will you go when the
rapture occurs? Will you be taken or left behind? Or what will
happen to you if you die before the rapture takes place?

What's Next for You?

As we ponder the future—both our own and that of the
world—the truth is that none of us knows how much time we
have *personally* or *prophetically*. It's one thing to know about the
future of the Middle East and the world, but it's much more
important for you to know about *your* future. Do you know
what will happen to you when you die or when the Lord comes?

The title of this book is *Middle East Burning*, and we have
used the metaphor of a raging grass fire to depict the revolutions that are sweeping the Middle East and North Africa. Let's
use that same metaphor to depict what the Lord has done for
each of us.

There's a well-known story about a group of early pioneers

who were making their way across the central United States to a distant place that had been opened up for homesteading. They traveled in covered wagons drawn by oxen, and progress was painfully slow. One day they were horrified to see a long line of smoke to the west, stretching for miles across the prairie, and soon it was apparent that the dried grass was burning fiercely and racing toward them. They had crossed a river the day before, but it would be impossible to go back all the way to the river before the flames would be upon them. One man seemed to have understanding as to what could be done. He gave the command to set fire to the grass behind them. Then when that area of grass was burned away, the whole company moved back upon it. As the flames roared on toward them from the west, a little girl cried out in terror, "Are you sure we shall not all be burned up?" The leader replied, "My child, the flames cannot reach us here, for we are standing where the fire has been!"

What a picture of the believer who is safe in Christ through faith in Him! We are standing where the fire has already been. When Jesus died on the cross, He bore the full brunt of the burning wrath of God against human sin. He became sin for us and paid the price for our full pardon from sin (2 Corinthians 5:21). He took the fire of God's judgment for us so that if we stand in Him by faith, we have nothing to fear. The price for our sins has been paid, and we are safe in Him, our refuge.

As an old poem says,

> On Him Almighty vengeance fell,
> That must have sunk a world to hell;
> He bore it for a chosen race,
> And thus became their hiding place. [1]

Have you taken your refuge in Him by trusting in Him and Him alone as your Savior? Why not do it now?

Knowing Where You're Going

Not long ago I received an email that contained the following story, which I have enjoyed greatly.

> In January, 2000, leaders in Charlotte, North Carolina, invited their favorite son, Billy Graham, to a luncheon in his honor. Billy initially hesitated to accept the invitation because of his struggle with Parkinson's disease—he was 86 years old. But the Charlotte civic leaders replied, "We don't expect a major address. Just come and let us honor you." So he agreed.

> After wonderful things were said about him, Dr. Graham stepped to the rostrum, looked at the crowd, and said, "I'm reminded today of Albert Einstein, the great physicist, who, this month has been honored by *Time* magazine as the Man of the Century. Einstein was once traveling from Princeton on a train, when the conductor came down the aisle, punching the tickets of each passenger. When he came to Einstein's row, Einstein reached into his vest pocket. He couldn't find his ticket, so he reached into other pockets. It wasn't in any of them, so he looked into his briefcase, but could not find it. Then he searched the empty seat next to him. He could not find the ticket. The conductor said, 'Dr. Einstein, I know who you are. We all know who you are. I'm certain you bought a ticket. Don't worry about it.' Einstein nodded appreciatively. The

conductor continued down the aisle punching tickets. As he was ready to move to the next car, he turned around and saw that the great physicist was down on his hands and knees, looking under his seat for the ticket. The conductor rushed back and said, 'Dr. Einstein, Dr. Einstein, don't worry, I know who you are. No problem. You don't need a ticket. I'm sure you bought one.' Einstein looked at him and said, 'Young man, I too, know who I am. What I don't know is where I'm going.'

Having said that, Billy Graham continued, "See the suit I'm wearing? It's a brand new suit. My wife, my children and my grandchildren were telling me I've gotten a little slovenly in my old age. I used to be a bit more fastidious. So I went out and bought a new suit for this luncheon and one more occasion. You know what that occasion is? This is the suit in which I'll be buried. But when you hear I'm dead, I don't want you to immediately remember the suit I'm wearing. I want you to remember this: *I not only know who I am, I also know where I'm going.*

Do you know who you are? Do you know where you're going? Make sure today by trusting in Jesus Christ as your Savior and Lord.

Appendix A:
Egypt and the King of the South
by John Walvoord

Appendix B:
A Proposed Chronology
of the End Times

Egypt and the King of the South
by John Walvoord

I n many of my books I like to include material from my mentors. This chapter was excerpted from Dr. Walvoord's classic *The Nations in Prophecy*, which was published in 1967. With all that's going on in our world today, it's good to hear from solid voices from the past. While I do not agree with everything Dr. Walvoord says, especially with regard to Daniel 11:40-45, I want to expose you to his work, which has helped shape and mold my views on Bible prophecy. The material here is used with permission from Dr. Walvoord's son, John E. Walvoord. I want to thank him for allowing me to include it in this book.

Egypt and the King of the South

For more than three thousand years before the birth of Christ, Egypt was one of the greatest civilizations of the ancient world. Although much of its history was shrouded in mystery until the last century, the careful research of archaeologists has now provided almost limitless material for Egyptology, the science of the history and culture of this great nation of the past. Both from the standpoint of world history as well as the Biblical point of view, no other nation in Africa has had such an impact upon the world as a whole. Long before Babylon became great or Greek civilization came into flower, Egypt was already a great nation with a culture, history, and literature of its own. Nourished by the rich Nile valley, a delta a dozen miles wide and extending more than 500 miles in length, the land of Egypt early became one of the important factors in Biblical history and a great political power in the Mediterranean scene.

First mention of Egypt is under its ancient name of Mizraim, one of the sons of Ham in Genesis 10:6. The name itself is in a dual number which some believe refers to the natural division of the country into upper and lower Egypt. The modern name Egypt is thought to have been derived from a king by the name of Egyptus, who reigned in 1485 B.C. However, this conclusion is challenged. The Egyptians themselves referred to their land as Kemet, which has the meaning, "the black land." In the Bible it is also referred to as "the land of Ham," referring to the Hamitic origin of the Egyptians.

First mention of Egypt in the history of the Old Testament occurs in Genesis 12, where it is recorded that Abraham, because of the famine in the land of Canaan, went to Egypt (Genesis 12:10). There he attempted to hide the fact that Sarah was his wife and called her his sister—a partial truth. Only by intervention of God, who plagued Pharaoh, was Sarah rescued from the possibility of being taken as a wife of Pharaoh, and Abraham and his wife were sent out of Egypt.

The subsequent fruit of this ill-fated venture into Egypt was that he brought Hagar back with him. She ultimately became the mother of Ishmael (Genesis 16:1-6), who became the progenitor of the Arabian tribes who caused Israel so much trouble in the years that followed. Isaac was forbidden to go down into the land of Egypt as Abraham had done (Genesis 26:2), but Ishmael, guided by his mother, took a wife from Egypt (Genesis 21:21). It was not until the time of Joseph that the children of Israel again entered the land of Egypt.

Israel's Sojourn in Egypt

The first prophecy concerning Egypt in Scripture is found in the important fifteenth chapter of Genesis, where God confirms His covenant with Abraham. This chapter becomes the cornerstone of fulfillment of the Abrahamic covenant as it relates to possession of the land ultimately to be possessed by Israel, defined as the area "from the river of Egypt unto the great river, the river Euphrates" (Genesis 15:18). The expression "the river of Egypt" is probably a reference to the small river which is the boundary between Egypt and Palestine known as Wady-el-Arish. Apart from its reference to Egypt the chapter is important for its vision of God as "a burning lamp," which some have taken as the first instance of the Shekinah glory, and for its enumeration of the important nations adjacent to Israel or occupying its land in ancient times. Ten nations are named in Genesis 15:19-21.

Of major importance in relation to prophecy relating to Egypt, however, is the statement made to Abraham in Genesis 15:13, 14: "Know of a surety that thy seed shall be a stranger in a land that is not theirs, and shall serve them; and they shall afflict them four hundred years; and also that nation, whom they shall serve, will I judge: and afterward shall they come out with great substance." Although Egypt is not named, it is inescapable that this is the reference intended by the term "land that is not theirs." Thus long before the children of Israel went down into Egypt, it was predicted that they would sojourn there and be afflicted for 400 years.

Considerable attention has been given to the question of the 400 years, as historical data does not necessarily support this idea. If Israel left Egypt at the time of the Exodus about 1440 B.C. as most conservative scholars have agreed, they actually were in Egypt approximately 210 years. How can this be explained?

On the basis of the chronology of Galatians 3:17, where it is stated that the law came 430 years after the promise, a reasonable chronology is provided by beginning the 430 years at the time that Abraham left Ur of Chaldees. From that point to the birth of Isaac was a period of approximately 30 years. From the birth of Isaac to the birth of Jacob was another 60 years. From the birth of Jacob until Jacob went down into Egypt was another 130 years. This computation provides at least one good explanation for this reference to 400 years in Genesis 15. This is confirmed by the Septuagint rendering of Exodus 12:40, 41 where the children of Israel are said to have sojourned in the land of Egypt and in the land of Canaan for 430 years. This early reference to the children of Israel sojourning in the land of Egypt is one of the important milestones in prophecy in the Old Testament.

The story of how Jacob and his family went to Egypt is

given in detail in Genesis, chapter 37 to chapter 50. The story's importance in the history of Israel is demonstrated in the fact that Genesis, which devotes only two chapters to the whole creation narrative and only one chapter to the entrance of sin into the human race, uses fourteen chapters to trace the history of Israel from the time of Joseph being sold as a slave until the time of his death. Egypt was to be the matrix in which Israel would grow from a family of 70 to a great nation of several million.

The Exodus from Egypt

The history of Israel and of Egypt makes clear that the affliction or servitude mentioned in Genesis 15:13 was not always severe. However, during the latter portion of their sojourn in Egypt, there was a change in dynasty of the "Shepherd Kings" known as the Hyksos, who dominated the scene for two hundred years, 1750-1570 B.C., and were in power at the time that Joseph came to Egypt. Their expulsion and the formation of the new empire beginning with Dynasty XVIII set the stage not only for Israel's period of great glory and the construction of vast buildings, but also the slavery of the people of Israel. Thutmose III, who reigned 1482-1450 B.C., conquered all of Palestine, and defeated the Hittites. Thutmose III was followed by Amenhotep II (1450-1425 B.C.), the Pharaoh with whom the children of Israel had to deal in connection with the Exodus. The subsequent decline of Egypt and her loosening grip on Palestine ultimately made possible the conquest of the land by the children of Israel without Egyptian interference.

Contributing to the confusion which arose in the reign

of Amenhotep II were the series of plagues inflicted upon the Egyptians recorded in the early chapters of Exodus. The story of Israel's deliverance from Egypt and the destruction of the Egyptian host in the Red Sea marks the close of the Egyptian bondage and the beginning of Israel as a separate nation.

The subsequent history of Egypt included constant contact with the children of Israel. The large part that Egypt played in the Old Testament is borne out by more than 700 references to Egypt in the Old Testament, contrasted to less than 30 in the New Testament. Most of these are reminders to Israel that they were "brought up out of the land of Egypt" and this recurring phrase occurs approximately 125 times.

Commercial relationships with Egypt reached a high point during the reign of Solomon. According to I Kings 3:1, "Solomon made affinity with Pharaoh king of Egypt, and took Pharaoh's daughter, and brought her into the city of David." I Kings 10:28 records that Egypt was the source of the horses Solomon used in his host of chariots for which he was famous. Solomon had 12,000 horsemen and 1400 chariots with both the horses and the chariots purchased out of Egypt (I Kings 10:26,29). Other commodities such as linen yarn were bought in Egypt. The commercial alliance with Egypt and Solomon's host of horses and chariots were in violation of the Word of God (Deuteronomy 17:16) and were a part of the secularization in Solomon's reign which led to Israel's spiritual downfall after his death.

Along with Assyria and Babylon, Egypt was one of the great nations of the past and is destined to have its important place in prophetic fulfillment at the end of the age. Egypt, however, was not the benefactor, but traditionally the enemy of Israel. This is seen in the sad commentary which forms a footnote to Solomon's relationships to Egypt recorded in the reign of Rehoboam, his successor, when Shishak king of Egypt conquered Jerusalem in the fifth year of the reign of Rehoboam and took away all of the treasures of the king's house and of the house of the Lord (I Kings 14:25, 26). Egypt, under the able leadership of the Egyptian ruler Pharaoh-Necho (609-593 B.C.), once again conquered Palestine during the reign of King Josiah (631-608 B.C.). The Egyptian bondage, however, was soon to end and be replaced by the Babylonian captivity with the rise of Nebuchadnezzar and the conquering of Jerusalem in 606 B.C. Jeremiah the prophet of the exile was carried against his will to Egypt, where he died. The Old Testament history does not record anything further of importance concerning Egypt. Where Biblical history stops, however, the prophetic narrative begins. Egypt was destined to have an important place in subsequent history as related to Israel and the Promised Land. The prophetic narrative concerning Israel is found in the great prophecies of Isaiah, Jeremiah, Ezekiel, and Daniel with echoes in the minor prophets Joel, Hosea, Micah, and Zechariah. To this the New Testament adds little of importance, but these great prophecies not only trace the subsequent history of Egypt, much of which has now been fulfilled, but also paint the picture of the final chapter in relation to the second coming of Christ.

The Prophecies of Isaiah Concerning Egypt

The prophecies of Isaiah include one of the more important

chapters of prophetic utterance concerning Egypt. The main section of this prophecy is found in the nineteenth chapter beginning with the ominous phrase "the burden of Egypt." The chapter is preceded by prophecies relating to Egypt's neighbor Ethiopia and is followed in chapter 20 by the prediction that Assyria would conquer Egypt and Ethiopia and lead them off as captives.

The nineteenth chapter of Isaiah is of special interest because it provides a rather comprehensive picture of God's plan and purpose for Egypt. The first half of the chapter predicts divine judgment upon Egypt. This will be fulfilled by the destruction of their idols (verse 1), destruction by civil war followed by the rule of "a cruel lord" and "a fierce king" (verses 2-4), judgment on the Nile River with attending economic distress (verses 5-10), and confusion of their wise men (verses 11-15), accompanied by a dread of Jehovah (verse 16). Divine judgment can well be associated with events of the Old Testament period, although it may be a foreshadowing also of future judgments.

Beginning with verse 16, however, the thought seems gradually to change to that which will be fulfilled in the future. Although they will experience fear of Judah (verses 16-18), it is predicted that there will be "an altar to the LORD in the midst of the land of Egypt, and a pillar at the border thereof to the LORD" (verse 19). The passage which follows seems to anticipate a time of blessing which may have its ultimate fulfillment in the millennial reign of Christ. The thought is summarized in verse 22 in the phrase "And the LORD shall smite Egypt: he shall smite and heal it: and they shall return even to the LORD, and he shall be intreated of them, and shall heal them." It is predicted that Egypt and Assyria will be associated with Israel as the three primary nations of that period and that a high-way will connect them (verses 23, 24). The prophecies which follow in chapter 20 refer to the historic invasion of Egypt by Assyria fulfilled largely in Isaiah's day. Because of the ultimate downfall of Egypt, Israel is exhorted not to trust in Egypt as a refuge against other enemies (Isaiah 30:2, 3; 31:1; 36:6, 9). These prophecies assure God's continued attention to the nation Israel and His divine judgment upon them for their sins. From the standpoint of unfulfilled prophecy, the most important passage in Isaiah is found in 11:10-16. Here Egypt is mentioned as one of the nations from which Israel will be regathered (11:11).

One of the interesting predictions is found in Isaiah 11:15, where it states, "And the LORD shall utterly destroy the tongue of the Egyptian sea; and with his mighty wind shall he shake his hand over the river, and shall smite it in the seven streams, and make men go over dryshod." The passage then goes on to mention the highway between Assyria and Egypt, also mentioned in Isaiah 19:23.

The interpretation depends largely on the question as to whether prophecy is to have literal fulfillment. Numerous attempts have been made to spiritualize these prophecies as referring to the progress of the church and conversion of the heathen. The more probable interpretation, however, is to take these as geographic terms and the events as those which will be related to the future Messianic kingdom. The tongue of the Egyptian Sea is clearly the northern end of the Red Sea. The prophecy then predicts that in this future time the topography of this land will be changed and what is now water will become dry land. This apparently is connected with the prophecy of a highway between Egypt and Israel, for which this may be a preparation.

This passage with its prediction of Israel's future place is set in the midst of prophecy that refers to the future millennial kingdom on earth. The first part of chapter 11 deals with Christ's reign on earth in perfect righteousness and equity. Chapter 12 refers to the joy and blessings that will characterize worship in this kingdom. It must be concluded therefore not only that Israel will be revived and that a future kingdom on earth will be realized, but that many of the ancient nations mentioned in the Bible will have their future revival as well. As Isaiah the prophet makes so plain in chapter 2, Jerusalem will be the capital of the world and the nations surrounding Israel will be subordinate but nevertheless blessed of God in that day. Taken as a whole, the prophecies of Isaiah set the pattern for other portions of the Word of God in tracing precise fulfillment of many prophecies in the past already fulfilled and establishing the main outline of Israel's future in relationship to the earthly kingdom of the Messiah.

The Prophecies of Jeremiah Concerning Egypt

Most of the prophecies of Jeremiah concern Jeremiah's own generation and the struggles of the kingdom of Judah with the contending powers of Babylon and Egypt. The possibility of a Babylonian conquest precipitated the choice of either casting their lot with Egypt or submitting to the Babylonian armies. It was in this situation that Jeremiah the prophet delivered his prophetic message. The good king Josiah had been succeeded by his son Jehoiakim, who was on the throne during the period in which Nebuchadnezzar was attempting to subdue Tyre—more than a dozen years. When Jehoiakim died, he was succeeded by his son Jehoiachin, who after three months was succeeded by Zedekiah, another son of Josiah and Jehoiachin's uncle. At this time Egypt was applying great pressure on the kingdom of Judah to cast their lot with them. When Jeremiah the prophet was consulted after receiving a message from God, he delivered his pronouncement as contained in Jeremiah 42. The substance of his reply was that they should not go down into Egypt and that if they did they would be destroyed. The advisors of King Zedekiah were intent, however, on going to Egypt and they rejected Jeremiah's prophetic warning and added insult to injury by forcing Jeremiah to accompany them, as indicated in Jeremiah 43. While in Egypt Jeremiah delivered a further message to the Jews (chapter 44) predicting their destruction except for a small remnant that would escape and return to Israel. The eloquent and moving plea of Jeremiah is prophetic literature at its best and is highly significant because it embodies also complete and literal fulfillment.

Jeremiah continues his prophetic utterances concerning Egypt in the series of prophecies against the Gentiles beginning in chapter 46 and concluding with the great section against Babylon in chapters 50 and 51. In these predictions he anticipates the defeat of Egypt by Nebuchadnezzar and the destruction of their great cities. The section on Egypt concludes in chapter 46:27, 28 with another reminder to Israel that Jacob need not be afraid, that Israel would return from their captivity and ultimately be at rest and ease in their own land. As Jeremiah concluded, "Fear thou not, O Jacob my servant, saith the LORD: for I am with thee; for I will make a full end of all the nations whither I have driven thee: but I will not make a full end of thee, but correct thee in measure; yet will I not leave thee wholly unpunished" (Jeremiah 46:28). Taken as a whole, Jeremiah does not contribute much to the future of Egypt except to assure God's continued and providential direction of this nation to the fulfillment of His purpose to bring Israel into their ancient land and establish them in the millennial kingdom.

The Prophecies of Ezekiel Concerning Egypt

The prophecies of Ezekiel include four long chapters dealing with Egypt, beginning with the prophecy against Pharaoh in chapter 29. Most of these predictions are concerning the domination of Egypt by Babylon and Nebuchadnezzar viewed as a divine judgment of God upon Pharaoh for claiming to be God and taking the credit for the fertility of the Nile Valley. With great prophetic eloquence, Ezekiel declares that Egypt is going to fall even as Assyria fell more than a century before. Most of chapter 31 is devoted to the analogy between the fall of Assyria and the fall of Egypt. The concluding prophecy concerning Egypt is a lamentation contained in chapter 32, in which Egypt is compared to a young lion trapped with a net and destroyed.

In a similar way miscellaneous other prophecies in Ezekiel relate to the downfall of Egypt. In the parable of the great eagle in Ezekiel 17 and its interpretation, Ezekiel declares that the king of Babylon has conquered Jerusalem and will judge those who flee to Pharaoh for refuge. The foolishness of relying on Egypt is again mentioned in Ezekiel 19:4. Israel is likewise denounced for their wickedness in idol worship in Egypt in the parable of Aholah and Aholibah, representing Samaria and Jerusalem. God's judgment upon them for this is declared.

Of these many prophecies most of them related to the contemporary situation of Ezekiel's day. The opening portion of chapter 30 of Ezekiel, however, referring as it does to the day of the Lord, has been interpreted as having a dual fulfillment, first, in the conquest of Egypt and Ethiopia by Babylon and, second, the future conquest of Egypt in the world struggle which will end the age. The main burden of the prophecy, however, seems to relate to Nebuchadnezzar and his conquest as indicated in Ezekiel 30:10. Taken as a whole, Ezekiel is an enlargement of the prophecies of Isaiah and Jeremiah depicting the judgment upon Egypt in his day, but assuring the people of Israel of their ultimate restoration and deliverance.

The Prophecies of Daniel Concerning Egypt

To the prophet Daniel was committed the major task of tracing the prophetic program of the four great world empires, namely, Babylon, Medo-Persia, Greece, and Rome. This in the main is the times of the Gentiles, constituting one of the major programs of God. Under the circumstances, it is surprising that Daniel has so little to say specifically about Egypt.

In Daniel 9:15 there is an allusion in Daniel's prayer to the deliverance of the people of Israel out of the land of Egypt, a constantly recurring thought in the Old Testament. In Daniel 11:8 there is mention of captives being carried into Egypt, a reference to the supremacy of Egypt during the reign of Ptolemy III Euergetes (246-222 B.C.).

The two other references to Egypt are found in Daniel 11:42, 43, and these relate to the future struggle among the nations at the end of the age still to be fulfilled.

The few direct references to Egypt, however, are misleading, as Egypt figures in a large way in the events both historic and prophetic described in Daniel chapter 11. Instead of referring to Egypt by name, reference is made instead to "the king of the south," an expression which occurs in Daniel 11:5, 6, 9, 11, 14, 15, 25, 29, 40, a total of ten references including the double reference in 11:25. Instead of referring to only one ruler, however, the expression in all probability concerns seven different kings of Egypt, six of them in the past and one still to come.

The period of history described in Daniel 11:5-20 was the tangled period subsequent to the death of Alexander the Great, which deals with the struggles of Egypt with the lands to the north, principally Syria. The accuracy of the prophecy given by Daniel more than two hundred years before it was fulfilled is so minute that liberal scholars reject the idea that Daniel could possibly have written it and claim it was written by a pseudo-Daniel after the events had actually taken place. Evangelical scholarship, however, has been agreed that this is genuine prophecy and another illustration of the accuracy of the prophetic Word.

The king of the south mentioned in Daniel 11:5 was probably Ptolemy I Soter (323-285 B.C.), who was associated with the famous Seleucus I Nicator (312-281 B.C.), who was king of Babylon. Their alliance succeeded in defeating Antigonus and Seleucus I Nicator became the ruler of the entire area from Asia Minor to India and hence was stronger than Ptolemy I Soter, his associate.

The king of the south mentioned in Daniel 11:6 was probably Ptolemy II Philadelphus (283-246 B.C.) who gave his daughter Berenice to Antiochus II Theos (261-246 B.C.) who was the third in the line of Seleucid kings.

Reference to another king of Egypt is found in verses 7 and 8. He was probably Ptolemy II Euergetes (246-222 B.C.), referred to as the king of the south in Daniel 11:9. The king of the south of Daniel 11:11 was Ptolemy IV Philopator (222-203 B.C). The king of the south mentioned in verse 14 and referred to under the term "the arms of the south" in verse 15 was Ptolemy V Epiphanes (204-181 B.C) who was an infant at the time of his accession. As Daniel 11:13-16 indicates, he was crushed by the great army of Antiochus III the celebrated ruler of Syria to the north in a battle at Paneiom in 198 B.C. The result was that Egypt lost its hold upon the Holy Land and it was transferred to the Seleucids. This set the stage for the activities of Antiochus Epiphanes described in Daniel 11:21-35 (previously discussed), which constitutes such a significant foreshadowing of the coming man of sin and world ruler in the end time. Antiochus III was followed by his son Seleucus IV Philopator (187-175 B.C.), to whom reference is made in Daniel 11:20 as a raiser of taxes. He was followed in turn by Antiochus Epiphanes.

The exact fulfillment of these many prophecies, including

that of Antiochus Epiphanes in Daniel 11:21-35, sets the stage for the climactic prophecy beginning in Daniel 11:36, which leaps the centuries to the end of the age and the final king of Gentile power.

Daniel 11:36-45 concerns itself with the military and political struggles of the end of the age with special reference to the great tribulation the last three-and-a-half years before the second coming of Christ to the earth. The period is described as "the time of the end" in verse 35 and again in Daniel 11:40. The description of the warfare which characterizes the period of Daniel 11:40-45 speaks of a future king of the south, namely, of Egypt engaging in a military campaign against the king of Daniel 11:36, who is most probably identified as the world ruler of the end time. At the same time there is an attack by the king of the north, namely, Russia and her associates as they contend with the world ruler for control of the Holy Land.

It is reasonable to assume from the description of a series of battles that this is not just one single military encounter, but a series of military maneuvers which come at the very end of the great tribulation. Earlier there may have been other wars such as that of Ezekiel 38 and 39 which led up to the world empire directed by the head of the revived Roman Empire. With the defeat of Russia described in Ezekiel 38 and 39, however, the Roman ruler becomes a world ruler. His empire accomplished by proclamation and because there was no suitable military force to contend against him does not stand indefinitely, however, and begins to fall apart with a major rebellion developing as the great tribulation closes. This is the scene described in Daniel 11:40 and following.

According to Daniel 11:40-42 the preliminary struggle results in the Roman ruler being victorious and conquering Egypt and putting down the king of the south. In the process, however, of assuming "power over the treasures of gold and of silver, and over all the precious things of Egypt" (Daniel 11:43) he receives word of additional problems of a military force coming from the east and from the north. This apparently refers to the great host coming from the Orient described first in Revelation 9:13-21, an army of two hundred million and then again in a later phase in the invasion described in Revelation 16:12-16. The great invasion from the east therefore follows the attack of the king of the south. Daniel 11, however, makes plain that in the preliminary struggle the Roman ruler is victorious as indicated in Daniel 11:45. However, at the very time of the second coming of Christ according to Zechariah chapter 14:1-3 a military struggle is going on in the city of Jerusalem itself and the armies of the world are gathered in the Holy Land with the valley of Megiddo referred to as Armageddon (Revelation 16:16) as its marshaling center.

From this entire context it is evident that the king of the south, namely, Egypt, has a part in end-time events and participates in the world struggle leading up to the second coming of Christ.

However, a final chapter is written in Egypt's future in which it is pictured that Egypt will have a spiritual revival (cp. Isaiah 19:18-24) and Israel will be regathered.

Prophecies of Egypt in the Minor Prophets

The few scattered references to Egypt in the minor prophets

do not contribute much to the total picture. Hosea has the most references, including the Messianic statement in Hosea 11:1: "When Israel was a child, then I loved him, and called my son out of Egypt." This reference to the Exodus is interpreted as having a dual meaning in that it prophesies that Jesus would come out of Egypt (cp. Matthew 2:15). Other references to Egypt in Hosea either predict destruction of those who go to Egypt as in Hosea 7:11-16 or contain warnings concerning returning to Egypt as in 8:13; 9:3, 6; 11:5. Joel 3:19 predicts that "Egypt shall be a desolation." This seems to be a general reference to God's judgment on Egypt largely already fulfilled although it is found in a passage dealing with Israel's millennial blessings.

Micah in one reference (7:12) predicts the regathering of Israel from Assyria and from "the fortress." This is best interpreted as a reference to Egypt and hence the prediction is that the children of Israel will be gathered from Assyria, the cities of Egypt ("the fortified cities"), and from Egypt ("the fortress") even to the river (the Euphrates). This reference to regathering from Egypt may presume an influx of Jews into Egypt which is not true today or it may refer to the few that are there as being subject to regathering.

The subject of regathering is brought up again in Zechariah 10:10, where it is stated concerning Israel, "I will bring them again also out of the land of Egypt, and gather them out of Assyria." Zechariah 10:11 refers to the fact that both Assyria and Egypt will be afflicted under divine judgment in contrast to God's blessing upon Israel.

The final reference in the Old Testament to Egypt is found

in Zechariah 14:18, 19, where in the future millennial kingdom it is stated, "And if the family of Egypt go not up, and come not, that have no rain; there shall be the plague, wherewith the LORD will smite the heathen that come not up to keep the feast of tabernacles. This shall be the punishment of Egypt, and the punishment of all nations that come not up to keep the feast of tabernacles." From these verses it may be concluded that God will continue to discipline Egypt even in the coming millennial kingdom if they have failed to obey Him and observe His feast.

Summary

Taking the Scriptural prophecies concerning Egypt as a whole, it is easily seen that Egypt has had a great role as one of the principal neighbors of Israel in centuries past. The fact that Israel sojourned in Egypt, grew to be a great nation there and subsequently had so many dealings with Egypt forms a large part of the Old Testament prophetic narrative.

The Scriptures, however, reveal that Egypt will also have a place in the future. Egypt will be one of the nations which figure in the final world conflict and will be the leader of the African forces in contending against the Roman ruler who is attempting to maintain a world empire. The role of Egypt will continue in the millennial kingdom after the searching divine judgments which attend the second coming. The last word of the Old Testament pictures the continued discipline of Egypt in the millennium if they fail to observe the rule of the king.

A Proposed Chronology of the End Times

In many of my books on end-times prophecy I like to include this outline at the end. I recognize that it's not easy trying to fit together all the pieces of the end times into a chronological sequence. This outline is my best attempt, at this time, to put the pieces together. I certainly wouldn't insist on the correctness of every detail in this outline, but my prayer is that it will help you get a better grasp of the overall flow of events in the end times.

I. Events in Heaven

   A. The Rapture of the Church (1 Corinthians 15:51-58; 1 Thessalonians 4:13-18; Revelation 3:10)

   B. The Judgment Seat of Christ (Romans 14:10; 1 Corinthians 3:9-15; 4:1-5; 9:24-27; 2 Corinthians 5:10)

   C. The Marriage of the Lamb (2 Corinthians 11:2; Revelation 19:6-8)

D. The Singing of Two Special Songs (Revelation 4–5)

E. The Lamb Receiving the Seven-Sealed Scroll (Revelation 5)

II. Events on Earth

A. Seven-year Tribulation

1. Beginning of the Tribulation

a. Seven-year Tribulation begins when the Antichrist signs a covenant with Israel, bringing peace to Israel and Jerusalem (Daniel 9:27; Ezekiel 38:8,11)

b. The Jewish temple in Jerusalem is rebuilt (Daniel 9:27; Revelation 11:1)

c. The reunited Roman Empire emerges in a ten-nation confederation (Daniel 2:40-44; 7:7; Revelation 17:12)

2. First Half (3 1/2 Years) of the Tribulation

a. The seven seal judgments are opened (Revelation 6)

b. The 144,000 Jewish believers begin their great evangelistic ministry (Revelation 7)

c. Gog and his allies invade Israel, while Israel is at peace under the covenant with Antichrist, and are supernaturally decimated by God (Daniel 11:40-45; Ezekiel 38–39). This will probably occur somewhere near the end of the 3 1/2-year period. The destruction of these forces will create a major shift in the balance of power that will enable the Antichrist to begin his rise to world ascendancy.

3. The Midpoint of the Tribulation

   a. Antichrist breaks his covenant with Israel and invades the land (Daniel 9:27; 11:40-41)

   b. Antichrist begins to consolidate his empire by plundering Egypt, Sudan, and Libya, whose armies have just been destroyed by God in Israel (Daniel 11:42-43; Ezekiel 38–39)

   c. While in North Africa, Antichrist hears disturbing news of insurrection in Israel and immediately returns there to destroy and annihilate many (Daniel 11:44)

   d. Antichrist sets up the abomination of desolation in the rebuilt Temple in Jerusalem (Daniel 9:27; 11:45a; Matthew 24:15; 2 Thessalonians 2:4; Revelation 13:5,15-18)

   e. Sometime during these events the Antichrist is violently killed, possibly as a result of a war or assassination (Daniel 11:45; Revelation 13:3,12,14; 17:8)

   f. Satan is cast down from heaven and

begins to make war with the woman,
Israel (Revelation 12:7-13); the chief
means he uses to persecute Israel is the
two beasts in Revelation 13

g. The faithful Jewish remnant flee to
Petra in modern Jordan, where they are
divinely protected for the remainder
of the Tribulation (Matthew 24:16-20;
Revelation 12:15-17)

h. The Antichrist is miraculously raised from
the dead to the awestruck amazement of
the entire world (Revelation 13:3)

i. After his resurrection from the dead, the
Antichrist gains political control over the
ten kings of the reunited Roman Empire;
three of these kings will be killed by the
Antichrist and the other seven will submit
(Daniel 7:24; Revelation 17:12-13)

j. The two witnesses begin their 3 1/2-year
ministry (Revelation 11:2-3)

k. Antichrist and the ten kings destroy
the religious system of Babylon and
set up their religious capital in the city
(Revelation 17:16-17)

4. Last Half (3 1/2 Years) of the Tribulation

a. Antichrist blasphemes God and the false
prophet performs great signs and wonders

and promotes false worship of the Antichrist (Revelation 13:5,11-15)

b. The mark of the beast (666) is introduced and enforced by the false prophet (Revelation 13:16-18)

c. Totally energized by Satan, the Antichrist dominates the world politically, religiously, and economically (Revelation 13:4-5,15-18)

d. The trumpet judgments are unleashed throughout the final half of the Tribulation (Revelation 8–9)

e. Knowing he has only a short time left, Satan intensifies his relentless, merciless persecution of the Jewish people and Gentile believers on earth (Daniel 7:25; Revelation 12:12; 13:15; 20:4)

5. The End of the Tribulation

a. The bowl judgments are poured out in rapid succession (Revelation 16)

b. The campaign of Armageddon begins (Revelation 16:16)

c. Commercial Babylon is destroyed (Revelation 18)

d. The two witnesses are killed by Antichrist and are resurrected by God 3 1/2 days later (Revelation 11:7-12)

      e. Christ returns to the Mount of Olives and slays the armies gathered against Him throughout the land, from Megiddo to Petra (Revelation 19:11-16; Isaiah 34:1-6; 63:1-5)

      f. The birds gather to feed on the carnage (Revelation 19:17-18)

B. After the Tribulation

  1. Interval or Transition Period of 75 Days (Daniel 12:12)

      a. The Antichrist and the false prophet are cast in the lake of fire (Revelation 19:20-21)

      b. The abomination of desolation is removed from the temple (Daniel 12:11)

      c. Israel is regathered (Matthew 24:31)

      d. Israel is judged (Ezekiel 20:30-39; Matthew 25:1-30)

      e. Gentiles are judged (Matthew 25:31-46)

      f. Satan is bound in the abyss (Revelation 20:1-3)

      g. Old Testament and Tribulation saints are resurrected (Daniel 12:1-3; Isaiah 26:19; Revelation 20:4)

  2. 1000-year Reign of Christ on Earth (Revelation 20:4-6)

3. Satan's Final Revolt and Defeat (Revelation 20:7-10)

4. The Great White Throne Judgment of the Lost (Revelation 20:11-15)

5. The Destruction of the Present Heavens and Earth (Matthew 24:35; 2 Peter 3:3-12; Revelation 21:1)

6. The Creation of the New Heavens and New Earth (Isaiah 65:17; 66:22; 2 Peter 3:13; Revelation 21:1)

7. Eternity (Revelation 21:9–22:5)

Notes

1. Billy Graham, *World Aflame* (New York: Doubleday, 1965), p. 1.

Chapter 1—Arab Spring...or Fall?

1. Yoram Ettinger, "Second Thought: US-Israel Initiative" (April 29, 2011), http://www.ynetnews
.com/articles/0,7340,L-4062310,00.html.

2. *Wall Street Journal* (October 19, 2006).

3. *The Jerusalem Post* (May 15, 2011), http://new.jpost.com/LandedPages/Subscribe.aspx.

4. *Newsweek* (March 28 and April 4, 2011).

5. *Time* (February 14, 2011).

6. *NPR* (February 10, 2011).

7. *The Economist* (February 10, 2011).

8. *The Wall Street Journal* (March 26, 2011).

9. *CNISS* (March 9, 2011).

10. *Time* (February 26, 2011).

11. *World* (April 9, 2011).

12. Gary G. Cohen, "The Middle East Today and the Parable of the Empty and Swept House," *Zion's Fire* (March-April 2011), 12.

13. Dirk Vandewalle, "After Gaddafi," *Newsweek* (March 7, 2011), 21.

14. Anup Shah, "Middle East and North Africa Unrest," *Global Issues* (April 6, 2011), www.global
issues.org/issue/103.

15. *The Omega Letter Intelligence Digest*, Vol: 115 Issue: 8 (Friday, April 08, 2011).

16. Ibid.

17. Ibid.

18. Ibid.

19. Ibid.

20. Roger Wiegand, "A World in Chaos: The Middle East Is Burning" (March 3, 2011), traderrog
.wordpress.com/2011/03/03/a-world-in-chaos-the-middle-east-is-burning.

21. Niall Ferguson, "The Mash of Civilizations," *Newsweek* (April 18, 2011), 9.

22. "A Golden Opportunity," *The Economist* (April 2, 2011), 22.

23. Ibid.

24. "Islam and the Arab Revolutions," *The Economist* (April 2, 2011), 11.

25. George Friedman. "Revolution and the Muslim World," *Stratfor Global Intelligence* (February 22, 2011), www.stratfor.com/weekly/20110221-revolution-and-muslims-world.

26. "Hamas leader on Nakba Day: The Zionist project must end," Haaretz.com (May 24, 2011).

27. Jill Nelson, "Neighborhood Watch," *World* (April 9, 2011), 40.

28. Ibid.

29. "A Golden Opportunity," *The Economist* (April 2, 2011), 22.

30. This was derived from Charles H. Dyer, *World News in Bible Prophecy* (Wheaton, IL: Tyndale House, 1993), 100.

31. Ben Feller, Face to Face "Netanyahu Rejects Obama on Borders," *Associated Press* (May 20, 2011), http://abcnews.go.com/Politics/wirestory?id/3644888.

32. Niall Ferguson, "The Revolution Blows Up," *Newsweek* (June 13 and 20, 2011), 8.

33. Ibid.

34. John F. Walvoord, *Armageddon, Oil and the Middle East Crisis: What the Bible says About the Future of the Middle East and the End of Western Civilization*, rev. ed. (Grand Rapids: Zondervan, 1990), 27.

35. Ibid.

36. John F. Walvoord, *The Nations in Prophecy* (Grand Rapids: Zondervan, 1967), 27.

Chapter 2—What's Next?

1. Jeff Brumley, "Global events, prophecy stir talk of 'End Time' beliefs" (July 16, 2012), jackson ville.com/.../2010-07-16/story/global-events-prophecy-stir-talk-end-beliefs.

2. "We need to bring End-times beliefs out of their closet" (November 8, 2008), www.canada.com/vancouversun/news/editorial/story.html?id=ac308456-5493-4756-8ad6-68d.

3. Amiram Barkat, "Statistics bureau: Israeli Jews outnumber Jews in the U.S.," Haaretz.com, www.haaretz.com/hasen/pages/ShArt.jhtml?

4. Ibid.

5. Randall Price, *Jerusalem in Prophecy: God's Final Stage for the Final Drama* (Eugene, OR: Harvest House, 1998), 220.

6. Charles H. Dyer, *World News and Bible Prophecy* (Wheaton, IL: Tyndale House, 1993), 61.

Chapter 3—The Four Power Blocs of the Future

1. John F. Walvoord, *Armageddon, Oil and the Middle East Crisis*, rev. ed. (Grand Rapids: Zondervan, 1974), 228.

2. "Iraq Suffers as the Euphrates River Dwindles," *The New York Times* (July 13, 2009), A1.

3. J. Dwight Pentecost, *Will Man Survive? The Bible Looks at Man's Future* (Grand Rapids: Zondervan, 1971), 119.

Chapter 4—The Coming Middle East War

1. Tim LaHaye and Jerry Jenkins, *Left Behind* (Wheaton, IL: Tyndale House, 1995), 14.

2. Bryanna Tidmarsh, "Israel deploys Iron Dome in Beersheba," *Bellarmine Concord* (March 30, 2011), www.theconcordonline.com/israel-deploys-iron-dome-in-beersheba-1.2469303.

3. Josephus, *Antiquities* 1.6.1.

4. C.F. Keil, *Ezekiel, Daniel, Commentary on the Old Testament*, trans. James Martin (Reprint; Grand Rapids: Eerdmans, 1982), 159. Wilhelm Gesenius, *Gesenius' Hebrew-Chaldee Lexicon to the Old Testament* (Reprint, Grand Rapids: Eerdmans, 1949), 752.

5. Clyde E. Billington, Jr. "The Rosh People in History and Prophecy (Part Two)," *Michigan Theological Journal* 3 (1992): 54-61.

6. G.A. Cooke, *A Critical and Exegetical Commentary on the Book of Ezekiel*, International Critical Commentary, eds. S.R. Driver, A. Plummer, and C.A. Briggs (Edinburgh: T. & T. Clark, 1936), 408-9. John Taylor agrees. He says, "If a place-name *Rosh* could be vouched for, RV's *prince of Rosh, Meshech, and Tubal* would be the best translation." John B. Taylor, *Ezekiel: An Introduction & Commentary*, Tyndale Old Testament Commentaries, gen. ed. D. J. Wiseman (Downers Grove, IL: InterVarsity Press, 1969), 244. Since it appears that there was a place in Ezekiel's day known as Rosh, this is the superior translation. For an extensive, thorough presentation of the grammatical and philological support for taking Rosh as a place name, see James D. Price, "Rosh: An Ancient Land Known to Ezekiel," *Grace Theological Journal* 6 (1985): 67-89.

7. Gesenius, *Gesenius' Hebrew and Chaldee Lexicon*, 752.

8. Billington, Jr. "The Rosh People in History and Prophecy (Part Two)," 145-46; Clyde E. Billington, Jr., "The Rosh People in History and Prophecy (Part Three)" *Michigan Theological Journal* 4 (1993): 59, 61; Price, "Rosh: An Ancient People Known to Ezekiel," 71-73; Jon Mark Ruthven, *The Prophecy that Is Shaping History* (Fairfax, VA: Xulon Press, 2003).

9. "Bashir: sharia law will be strengthened if South Sudan votes to secede" (www.csmonitor.com/World/Africa/Africa-Monitor/2010/1223/Bashir-sharia-law-will-be).

10. Josephus, *Antiquities* 1.6.1.

11. Some argue that the weapons mentioned in Ezekiel 38–39 do not fit with a future, last days' time frame. The weapons mentioned in Ezekiel 38–39 are ancient weapons that are made out of wood, such as bows, arrows, shields, war clubs, and spears (39:9). And the means of transportation is horses (38:15).

    What about the weapons that are used in this invasion? How do we account for the use of ancient weapons if this invasion takes place during the end times? There are two plausible solutions to this problem. First, it could be that by the time this event is fulfilled that nations will have to resort back to archaic weapons and means of transportation due to oil shortages and other wars that depleted the resources of these nations. A second explanation is that Ezekiel spoke, inspired by the Holy Spirit, in language that the people of that day could understand. If he had spoken of planes, missiles, tanks, and rifles, this text would have been nonsensical to everyone until the twentieth century. Moreover, the main point of Ezekiel's great prophecy is that a specific group of nations will attack Israel with the intent of completely destroying her. The focus clearly is not the specific weapons that will be used by these invaders. Rather, the prophet is pointing out that weapons of destruction will be used by the invaders, and that there will be all-out warfare. This is not symbolic interpretation, but rather, understanding God's Word in its historical context as understood by the original audience. The Holy Spirit speaks to people in their own context and culture in ways that communicate God's truth in a meaningful, understandable manner.

12. John Phillips, *Exploring the Future: A Comprehensive Guide to Bible Prophecy*, 3rd ed. (Grand Rapids: Kregel, 2003), 343.

13. John Phillips, *Exploring the Future*, 347-48.

14. Luke Baker, "Israel Asks Itself the $150 Billion Question," Reuters.com (May 25, 2011).

Chapter 5—Egypt and the Rise of the King of the South

1. This quote is attributed to Henry Kissinger and is said to have originated in commentary he offered during the 1970s with regard to the Middle East.

2. John F. Walvoord, *The Nations in Prophecy* (Grand Rapids: Zondervan, 1967), 133.

3. Hal Lindsey, *The Late Great Planet Earth* (Grand Rapids: Zondervan, 1970), 72-73.

4. J. Dwight Pentecost, *Will Man Survive? The Bible Looks at Man's Future* (Grand Rapids: Zondervan, 1971), 119.

5. Charles C. Ryrie, *The Best Is Yet to Come* (Chicago: Moody Press, 1981), 63.

6. Lindsey, *The Late Great Planet Earth*, 77.

7. "Poll: More than half of Egyptians want to cancel peace treaty with Israe," *The Associated Press* (April 26, 2011), www.haaretz.com/.../poll-more-than-half-of-egyptians-want-to-cancel-peace-treaty-with-israel.

8. "Egypt Boils Over," *Newsweek* (August 1 and 8, 2011), http://www.thedailybeast.com/news week/2011/07/24/egypt-s-angry-electorate.html.

9. David D. Kirkpatrick, "In Shift, Egypt Warms to Iran and Hamas, Israel's Foes," *The New York Times* (April 28, 20, 2011), http://topics.nytimes.com/top/news/international/countriesandter ritories/egypt/index.html.

10. Fareed Zakaria, "The Revolution," *Time* (February 14, 2011), 35.

11. Dennis Prager, "Eight Reasons Not to Be Optimistic About Egypt" (March 1, 2011), www.den nisprager.com/columns.aspx. Used with permission.

12. David D. Kirkpatrick and J. David Goodman, "Muslim Brotherhood in Egypt to Be Political Party," *The New York Times* (February 15, 2011), www.nytimes.com/2011/02/16/world/middle east/16brotherhood.html?_r=1&sq=%22muslim%20brotherhood%20in%20egypt%20to%20 be%20political%20party%22&st=cse#.

13. John F. Walvoord, *Daniel: The Key to Prophetic Revelation* (Chicago: Moody Press, 1971), 252.

14. Joyce Baldwin, *Daniel: An Introduction and Commentary*, Tyndale Old Testament Commentaries, gen. ed. D.J. Wiseman (Downers Grove, IL: InterVarsity Press, 1978), 184.

15. Warren Wiersbe, *Be Resolute* (Colorado Springs: Cook Communications, 2000), 131.

16. H.A. Ironside, *Lectures on Daniel the Prophet* (Neptune City, NJ: Loizeaux Brothers, 1911), 191-92.

17. Leon J. Wood, *A Commentary on Daniel* (Grand Rapids, MI: Zondervan, 1973), 280.

18. John C. Whitcomb, *Daniel* (Chicago: Moody Press, 1985), 148; Donald K. Campbell, *Daniel: God's Man in a Secular Society* (Grand Rapids: Discovery House, 1988), 162.

19. Leon Wood provides an excellent summary of the arguments for viewing these two passages as parallel in his book *A Commentary on Daniel*, 309.

20. Ryrie, *The Best Is Yet to Come*, 69.

21. This quote is attributed to Henry Kissinger and is said to have originated in commentary he offered during the 1970s with regard to the Middle East.

22. J. Vernon McGee, *Thru the Bible,* vol. 3 (Nashville, TN: Thomas Nelson, 1982), 244.

23. Wilbur M. Smith, *Egypt in Biblical Prophecy* (Boston: W. A. Wilde Company, 1957), 241-42.

24. McGee, *Thru the Bible*, vol. 3, 244.

25. Smith, *Egypt in Biblical Prophecy*, 242.

Chapter 6—Libya's Last Days

1. "The Craziest Guy in the Room: A Portrait of Gaddafi by Platon" (February 25, 2011), lightbox .time.com/2011/03/25/the-craziest-guy-in-the-room-a-portrait-of-gaddafi-by-platon.

2. Bobby Ghosh, "Gaddafi's Last Stand," *Time* (March 7, 2011), www.time.com/time/magazine/ article/0.9171.2055193-1,00.html.

3. John Phillips, *Exploring the Future: A Comprehensive Guide to Bible Prophecy*, 3rd ed. (Grand Rapids: Kregel, 2003), 339.

4. Ibid., 339-40.

5. Dirk Vandewalle, "Good Riddance, Gaddafi," *Newsweek* (September 5, 2011), 38.

6. Ken Stier, "Would Gaddafi's Fall Really Bring Peace to Libya?" *Time* (February 25, 2011), 18.

7. Niall Ferguson, "In Gaddafi's Wake: The dictator's fall is proof that America can topple a rogue regime. What comes next may underscore our impotence," *Newsweek* (September 5, 2011), 6.

8. "Former jihadist at the heart of Libya's revolution," CNN.com at http:/cnn.site.printhis.click ability.com/pt/cpt?expire=&title&=Former+jihadist+at+at+the+heart.

9. John Phillips, *Exploring the Future: A Comprehensive Guide to Bible Prophecy,* 3d ed. (Grand Rapids: Kregel, 2003), 343.

Chapter 7: Northern Storm: Russia, Turkey, and Iran

1. As cited by Joel Rosenberg at www.joelrosenberg.com/ezekiel-q9.asp.

2. Adrian Blomfield, "Russia Is Returning to a State of Tyranny" (November 22, 2006), telegraph. co.uk; Ethan S. Burger, "The Price of Russia's 'Dictatorship of Law,'" *The Christian Science Monitor* (October 12, 2006), www.csmonitor.com/2006/1012/p09301-coop.html. Political scientist Arnold Beichman has dubbed Putin "Stalin lite."

3. Sebnem Arsu, "Turkey's Pact with Russia Will Give It Nuclear Plant," *The New York Times* (May 12, 2011), www.nytimes.com/2010/05/13/world/europe/13turkey.html.

4. Jill Nelson, "Streetcar democracy," *World* (May 7, 2011), 53.

5. Ibid.

6. Ibid.

7. "Ankara in the Middle," www.newsweek.com/2010/07/26/ankara-in-the-middle.html.

8. Susan Fraser and Matti Friedman, "Turkey Downgrades Israeli Ties, Expels Envoy over Flotilla Raid," *The Daily Oklahoman* (September 3, 2011), 7A.

9. Jill Nelson, "Streetcar democracy," *World* (May 7, 2011), 58.

10. Nelson, "Streetcar democracy," 52.

11. Sam Dagher, "Turkey Reveals Quiet Rebel Payments," *The Wall Street Journal* (August 24, 2011), A8.

12. Owen Matthews, "Eastern Star" *Newsweek* (September 11, 2010), www.newsweek.com/2010/09/11/should-turkey-s-erdogan-worry-the-west.html.

13. Niall Ferguson, "The Mideast's Next Dilemma: With Turkey flexing its muscles, we may soon face a revived Ottoman Empire," *Newsweek* (June 27, 2011), 6.

14. Ibid.

15. Matthews, "Eastern Star."

16. *Wall Street Journal* (October 19, 2006).

17. "Ahmadinejad: the Era of Zionism Is Over" (April 18, 2011), www.jpost.com/MiddleEast/Article.aspx?id=217081.

18. See at thinkexist.com/quotes/mahmoud_ahmadinejad.

19. "Ahmadinejad: the Era of Zionism Is Over."

20. Anton La Guardia, "Divine Mission Driving Iran's New Leader" (January 14, 2006), telegraph.co.uk/news/main.jhtm.

21. Thomas Erdbrink, "Ahmadinejad Criticized for Saying Long-Ago Imam Mahdi Leads Iran" (May 8, 2008), www.washingtonpost.com/wp-dyn/content/article/2008/05/07/AR2008050703587.html.

22. Scott Keyes, "In Midst of Libya Conflict, Bolton Argues for New War In Iran: 'Got to Walk and Chew Gum At the Same Time,'" *Progressive News Daily* (March 26, 2011), (www.progressivenewsdaily.com/?p=13839.

23. Joel C. Rosenberg, "Understanding Egypt, the Twelfth Imam, and the End of Days" (February 9, 2011), joelrosenberg.com.

24. Erick Stakelbeck, "Iranian Video Says Mahdi Is 'Near'" (March 28, 2011), http://www.cbn.com/cbnnews/world/2011/March/Iranian-Regime-Video-Says-Mahdi-is-Near.

25. Ibid.; Jonathon M. Seidl, "'The Coming Is Near': New Eerie Iran Propaganda Vid Trumpets Imminent Return of the 12th Imam" (March 28, 2011), www.theblaze.com/stories/new-iran-probaganda-vid-trumpets-immenent-return-of-12th-imam-the-coming-is-near.

26. Seidl, "The Coming Is Near."

27. Ibid.

28. "Davos panel sees huge Iranian response to attack" (January 29, 2011), news.yahoo.com/s/ap/20110128/ap_on.../eu_davos_forum_iran.

29. General Jerry Boykin, Epicenter Conference, San Diego, April 4, 2009.

Chapter 8—What About the Psalm 83 War?

1. Kate Ravilious, "Medieval Christian Book Discovered in Ireland Bog," *National Geographic News* (July 26, 2006), news.nationalgeographic.com/news/2006/07/060726-ireland-psalms .html.

2. Ibid.

3. Bill Salus, *Isralestine: The Ancient Blueprints of the Future Middle East* (Crane, MO: HighWay, 2008), 52.

4. Ibid., 6.

5. Salus identifies the Hagrites with the Egyptians because of the similarity between the name Hagar (Abraham's Egyptian concubine) and Hagrites. This view is not well supported. According to Assyrian inscriptions, the Hagrites were "a nomadic tribe living east of the Jordan." This identification is supported by 1 Chronicles 5:10. The Reubenites, who lived east of the Jordan River, did not fight the Egyptians who were far to the south, but nomadic tribes from their own area east of the Jordan (see also 1 Chronicles 5:20-22). Willem A. Van Gemeren, "Psalms," in *The Expositor's Bible Commentary*, gen. ed. Frank E. Gaebelein, vol. 5 (Grand Rapids: Zondervan, 1991), 539; Eugene H. Merrill, "1 Chronicles," in *The Bible Knowledge Commentary*, ed. John F. Walvoord and Roy B. Zuck (Wheaton, IL: Victor Books, 1985), 597.

6. Salus, *Isralestine*, 20.

7. Ibid.

8. Van Gemeren, "Psalms," 539.

9. Warren W. Wiersbe, *Be Worshipful: Glorifying God for Who He Is, Psalms 1-89* (Colorado Springs: David C. Cook, 2004), 263-64.

10. Derek Kidner, *Psalms 73-150: A Commentary*, Tyndale Old Testament Commentaries, gen. ed. D.J. Wiseman (Downers Grove, IL: InterVarsity Press, 1975), 300.

11. James Montgomery Boice, *Psalms*, vol. 2 (Grand Rapids: Baker Books, 1996), 682.

Chapter 9—Will Syria Be Destroyed Soon?

1. This quote is attributed to Henry Kissinger and is said to have originated in commentary he offered during the 1970s with regard to the Middle East.

2. Khaled Yacoub Oweis, "Assad holds Syria army despite Sunni-Alawite divide" (April 6, 2011), www.reuters.com/article/2011/04/06/us-syria-army-idUSTRE73543X20110406.

3. Mitchell Bard, "Potential Threats to Israel: Syria" (February 24, 2011), www.jewishvirtuallibrary .org/jsource/Threats_to_Israel/Syria.html.

4. Oweis, "Assad holds Syria army despite Sunni-Alawite divide."

5. Zeina Karam, "Hezbollah leader stands firm behind Syria," msnbc.com (May 25, 2011).

6. "IAEA: Syria site was 'very likely' an atom reactor," Reuters.com (May 24, 2011).

7. Bard, "Potential Threats to Israel: Syria."

8. Ibid.

9. Edmund Sanders, "Israel fears the alternative if Syria's Assad falls," *Los Angeles Times* (March 30, 2011), www.latimes.com/2011/mar/30/world/la-fg-israel-syria-20110331.

10. "Isaiah 17: Destruction of Damascus," www.raptureready.com/featured/gillette/Isaiah_17.html.

11. This quote is attributed to Henry Kissinger and is said to have originated in commentary he offered during the 1970s with regard to the Middle East.

Chapter 10—Where's America?

1. John F. Walvoord, *The Nations in Prophecy* (Grand Rapids: Zondervan, 1967), 175.

2. Charles C. Ryrie, *The Best Is Yet to Come* (Chicago: Moody, 1981), 109-10.

3. *World*, March 22-29, 2008, 18. This statistic comes from a report from the Centers for Disease Control and Prevention.

4. David Klepper, "Gay-relationship debates at turning point?" *The Daily Oklahoman* (May 29, 2011), 10A.

5. Jeffrey M. Jones, "Americans' Outlook for U.S. Morality Remains Bleak: Three-quarters say moral values in U.S. are getting worse" (May 17, 2012), www.gallup.com/poll/128042/Americans-Outlook-Morality-Remains-Bleak.aspx.

6. See www.bartleby.com/73/334.html.

7. Rich Miller and Simon Kennedy, "G-20 Shapes New World Order with Lesser Role for U.S. Markets," Bloomberg (April 3, 2009). www. bloomberg.com/apps/news?pid=newsarchive&sid=axEnb_LXw5yc.

8. Nick Gillespie, *"News Flash: Entitlement Spending Grows Like Giant Cancer on U.S. Economy"* (January 25, 2010), reason.com/blog/2010/01/25/news-flash-entitlement-spending.

9. Niall Ferguson, "An Empire At Risk," *Newsweek* (December 7, 2009), 44.

10. Ibid.

11. Ibid., 42, 44.

12. Ibid., 44.

13. Mona Charen, "Obama less than friendly toward Isreal," *The Daily Oklahoman* (May 25, 2011), 11A.

14. Ben Feller, "Face to Face, Netanyahu Rejects Obama on Borders," *(*May 20, 2011), news.yahoo.com/s/ap/us_obama_mideast.

15. Charen, "Hardly a Friend to Israel."

Chapter 11—Scanning the Horizon

1. Jehoida Brewer, *Gospel Magazine* (October 1776).

Other Good Harvest House Books by Mark Hitchcock

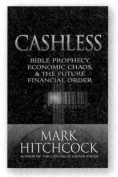

CASHLESS

Over 1900 years ago, the Bible predicted that one man, the coming Antichrist, will take control of the entire world's economy. Many have wondered how this could ever happen. We may now have the answer.

Today's worldwide financial chaos, global interdependency, and modern technology are all converging in such a way that a cashless society and one-world economy are not only possible, but inevitable.

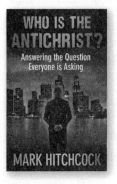

WHO IS THE ANTICHRIST?

Curiosity about the Antichrist is at an all-time high. As more and more people sense we are drawing nearer to the end times, they're asking who the Antichrist is, what he will do, and when he will arrive. This question-and-answer guide provides a fascinating tour of all the Bible's key passages about the Antichrist. You'll learn what you can know with certainty and how it affects your life right now.

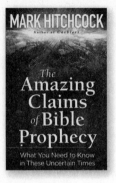

THE AMAZING CLAIMS OF BIBLE PROPHECY

At the time it was written, more than one-fourth of the Bible had predictions about the future. And over time, literally hundreds of those prophecies have been fulfilled with 100 percent accuracy.

Why so much attention on what is yet to come? This book will help you marvel over fascinating prophecies God has fulfilled down to every last detail, defend the Bible against those who doubt its truth claims, and recognize the important clues that indicate Earth's final hour is drawing near.

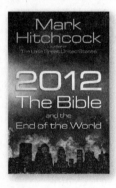

2012, THE BIBLE, AND THE END OF THE WORLD

The ancient Mayans were expert astronomers, and their advanced calendar cycles end on December 21, 2112. This has spurred widespread speculation that 12/21/12 will be a catastrophic day of apocalypse for the entire globe. The doomsday scenarios include destructive solar storms, massive earthquakes, a polar shift of the earth's magnetic fields, and total annihilation.

Missing from all the furor is a biblical perspective. This book considers the evidence, and holds it to the light of God's Word for answers we can trust.

THE MAYAN APOCALYPSE (A NOVEL)

Coauthored with Alton Gansky

The self-proclaimed Mayan descendant Robert Quetzal, media guru to the vulnerable, has taken Mayan prophecy claims to the extreme. Not only does he teach the end of the earth will come on December 21, 2012, he also offers a way out—for a price.

Andrew Morgan, a wealthy oil executive who has lost his family in a plane crash, is mad at God. Devastated by the tragedy, he puts his faith in Robert Quetzal and the ancient Mayan predictions. In his quest for answers, he meets Lisa Campbell, a smart, intuitive journalist researching the Mayan calendar. Lisa thinks the 2012 theories are nonsense and doesn't hesitate to say so. Morgan dismisses her when he learns she is a Christian.

As December 21, 2012 draws closer, a meteorite impact in Arizona, a volcanic eruption in Mexico, and the threat of an asteroid on a collision course with the earth escalate fears. Are these indicators of a global collapse? Will anyone survive? Does the Bible have the answers? Or has fate destined everyone to a holocaust from which there is no escape?